CW00405707

THE JOURNEY OF THE HERO

Personal Growth, Deep Ecology and the Quest for the Grail

FRIEDEMANN WIELAND

Published in Great Britain 1991 by

PRISM PRESS
2 South Street
Bridport
Dorset DT6 3NQ

Distributed in the USA by
AVERY PUBLISHING GROUP
120 Old Broadway
Garden City Park
NY 11040

Published in Australia by
UNITY PRESS
Lindfield
NSW 2070

ISBN 1 85327 048 2

© 1986 German edition, Kösel-Verlag
© 1991 Friedemann Wieland

All rights reserved. No part of this publication may be reproduced, stored in a retrieval system, or transmitted, in any form or by any means, electronic, mechanical, photocopying, recording or otherwise, without the prior permission of the publishers.

Typeset by Prism Press, Bridport, Dorset.
Printed by The Guernsey Press Ltd, The Channel Islands.

Acknowledgements

The idea for this book evolved from my work with Anne Morris Wieland. Our friendship and our search for contemporary rituals of transformation have led us on long journeys into many cultures. Important inspiration came from encounters with healers, shamans, dancers and musicians. My heartfelt gratitude goes to all of them.

I also wish to thank the friends and colleagues who supported and encouraged me and gave important inspiration: Jean Houston, Paul Rebillot, Florian Fricke, and many others.

Contents

Introduction

by Joanna Macy

Modern society has cut us off from our past, from a wisdom that can heal and guide. From every side come summons to get the 'newest', the 'latest', the most novel, unprecedented, up-to-the-minute allurement. That is hardly surprising, since our economy is fuelled by cravings; but in the process we become disinherited. Like the abducted or enchanted son of a king who grows up as a beggar, unaware of the wealth he could claim as his own, we have forgotten what is rightfully ours.

Now and again, however, into our midst come those who not only know the real riches of our inheritance, but who, portraying them in meaningful, modern idiom, can let us re-appropriate them. Then — with relief and recognition — we say, 'Oh yes, that is what it's like, that is my story.' Joseph Campbell is one of these, and so is Friedemann Wieland. They turn the key in the door and invite us to walk out into wider perspectives on our lives, and place our solitary journeys in larger, enlivening contexts. 'Oh, I've been here before,' we realise, 'My private pains are part of a bigger story; others have walked this path, known the griefs I experience, found the fulfilment I seek.'

The Legend of the Holy Grail has great power for the Western mind. Many features of this story strike a chord with our own situation today. There is the character of Parzifal himself; ready to venture, but confused and often at a loss, he reminds me of our own foolishness in this critical era — a foolishness that can save us when we acknowledge it. There, classically portrayed, is the wasteland — and also the ruler who, like his domain, has lost the powers of regeneration. And there are the questions that Parzifal is finally bold enough to ask. Bringing us to consciousness, they break the evil spell and return us to our innate vitality and sanity.

For the wealth of inherited wisdom to be incorporated, and especially the treasure house of mythology, simple cognitive recounting is insufficient. To be harvested, it must be accessed experientially. Friedemann Wieland knows how to make this happen. For he is an artist and therapist as well as a cultural historian, and able to tap many dimensions of our being. Among the most rewarding and unique features of this book are the guided experiences that propel us into the truth of the ancient myths and rites, and let us possess them as our own. With them I have recognized and danced with the dark witch Cundry, ambushed the complacencies of my Parzifal innocence, explored the promises of my own androgyny — and emerged stronger and lighter. I came out readier to embrace more aspects of myself and my world.

I am grateful, therefore, that the English-language publication of this book will bring its adventures and insights to many more of my fellow-beings. More is at stake now than our personal fulfilment. There is a world to be healed, a world in pain and in process of destruction. The beauty of Friedemann's vision, and indeed its truth, is that the ancient rite of initiation is still relevant, still ours to make, for our own joy and for the sake of all beings.

Prologue: The Uninvited Gods

In both myths and fairy tales we find ancient knowledge about the human condition — about ourselves. Myths and fairy tales are collective dreams. They speak of the issues and questions that touch us most closely. Through images they tell us about the creative forces of the soul and also about the enchantments and injuries which can slow life in its course.

In myths, such an enchantment can be an illness or a physical or emotional flaw. It can be a knot in a person's thread of life, great poverty, injustice, or a curse by which the wells dry up and the land can bear no more fruit. To free life from stagnation, a hero or a heroine will then enter on a journey into the world.

In many stories such enchantments are brought about by an uninvited god or goddess. The Battle for Troy began with a party, to which all the gods were invited — except the Goddess of Discord. In the fairy tale of Briar Rose, it was the uninvited thirteenth fairy who caused the princes, and with her the whole castle, to fall into a hundred-year sleep — into deep unconsciousness:

For the baptism of his child a king invited the wise women of his kingdom. There were thirteen wise women, but as the king had only twelve golden plates, one of the women was not invited. The wise women bestowed their magic gifts upon the child: they gave virtue, beauty, everything a person could wish for. But suddenly the thirteenth wise woman entered the hall and cried with a loud voice: 'The King's daughter shall in her fifteenth year prick herself with a spindle, and fall down dead!' Without another word she left the party. As the twelfth woman had not yet made her wish, she was able to soften the blow. The girl should not die from the spindle, but should fall into one hundred years of sleep.

The King at once had all spindles banned from his kingdom. On her fifteenth birthday, however, the princess discovered in a tower of the castle an old woman who was spinning at a wheel. When the girl touched the spindle she fell into a deep sleep:

> '... and this sleep extended over the whole palace; the King and Queen who had just come home, and had entered the great hall, began to sleep, and the whole of the court with them. The horses, too, went to sleep in the stable, the dogs in the yard, the pigeons upon the roof, the flies on the wall; even the fire that was flaming on the hearth became quiet and slept, the roast meat left off frizzling, and the cook, who was just going to pull the scullery boy's hair because he had forgotten something, let him go and went to sleep. And the wind fell, and on the trees before the castle not a leaf moved again. But round about the castle there began to grow a hedge of thorns, which became higher every year, and at last grew close up round the castle and all over it ...'
>
> (Jacob and Wilhelm Grimm: *Fairy Tales)*

The uninvited gods are an archetypal theme in many myths and legends. In symbolic form they represent essential forces and impulses that we suppress. they are the parts of ourselves that we send into exile; forces within us that want to enter into consciousness and want to be experienced and honored as gods.

The uninvited gods are the dreams that we do not dream, the songs that we do not sing, the dances that remain undanced. They are the parts of us that we cannot accept: the feelings we shut off, the unfulfilled desires and the unsuffered pain, the tears we do not cry, the love we have missed and the suppressed anger and hurt that we meet by becoming emotionally hard.

Whenever people invite these 'gods', when they celebrate and honor their life forces, life can reveal itself in great diversity and fullness. Even suffering loses its threatening character: it becomes a doorway to inner depths. But if we turn away and oppose these forces of life, we make them into uninvited gods and push them deep into the unconscious.

From here, these gods have a great deal of power. They threaten the apparent balance in which there seems to be no place for them. Dreams can then turn into nightmares. The springs dry up, songs become silent and inner rigidity prevents all movement.

To realize themselves in human consciousness, these gods will knock, in the shape of crises, at the door of our awareness. Myths and legends tell of such crises in which uninvited gods — like the thirteenth fairy — return from exile to claim their place in a person's consciousness. The story of Dionysos is an excellent example of an uninvited god returning to claim his rights.

Dionysos, God of Ecstasy and Chaos, is a brother of the Sun God, Apollo. While Apollo is a god of order, Dionysos is chaotic, able to lead a person beyond the limits of all order. Both gods demand worship and tribute. Whenever people barred one of them from their awareness, the god would realize himself more powerfully in their destiny. In 'The Bacchae' Euripedes tells the story of Dionysos.

Semele, his mother, once met the god Zeus in a forest and found great pleasure in him. Zeus, who was always open to encounters with mortals, made love with her in the forest. In bliss Semele returned to her sisters. She told them that she had made love with a god and that she would give birth to a god. But her sisters only laughed at her. They thought that she had been taken advantage of by a shepherd who had claimed to be a god. If she really had slept with a god, she should go back and ask him to reveal himself in his full divine power.

Semele returned confused to the forest and asked Zeus to reveal his true face. She wanted to feel him in the same way as did his wife, Hera, and she wanted to know if the

The Dance of Dionysos (from Maria-Gabriele Wosien: Tanz im Angesicht der Götter, *München, Kösel, 1986).*

child she expected was really a god. Zeus warned the girl because he knew that his power would kill her; but when Semele insisted on her wish, he revealed his full power in the form of lightning. Semele died instantly.

Zeus took the divine child from Semele's womb and sewed it in his thigh, where he carried it for the full term. When the young god was born, Zeus gave him to Hermes, who brought him to Asia to a nurse who raised him.

When Dionysos grew older he travelled through many countries, teaching people dance and the cultivation of wine. His arts spread fast, and accompanied by the sound of flutes and drums and followed by wildly dancing women (the Maenads), Dionysos returned to his home town of Thebes. But the people of Thebes worshipped Apollo, and there seemed no place for the wild god who demanded to be worshipped as well. Dionysos spoke to the people, 'You sent me into exile once before when you refused to believe my mother. I will forgive you, if you will now recognize and worship my divinity in Thebes. I will teach you a dance to carry you far beyond anything that you have ever dreamt of. If you will dance this dance in my honor, I shall be satisfied and move on. But if you deny me your worship, if you are not prepared to dance this — my lesser dance — than I will let you dance the greater dance of Dionysos — the dance of madness.'

Pentheus, the ruler of Thebes, despised the young god with his jubilantly Bacchic followers and denied him a place in Thebes. He ordered the god to be put into chains and brought into the deepest dungeon of his castle. At the command of Dionysos, however, an earthquake split the walls and the god reappeared, more magnificent than ever and covered in ivy, in the midst of his followers.

For Pentheus and his people now began the Greater Dance of Dionysos. Foolishly, the rich patrician women followed the god into the woods. They grew drunk on wild wine, they screamed and danced and celebrated ecstatic orgies. Covered with ivy, they swung the Thyrsos (a staff made from the Nortex bush, with a stone pine at its top), and accompanied by flutes, cymbals and tambourines they began the wild dance.

Finally, even Pentheus had become curious, and in disguise he followed the women into the woods. But when the women discovered the man, they thought they saw a lion and threw themselves at him and tore him to pieces. His own mother called for the murder, and mistakenly carried the head on a rod through the town, realizing only too late that this was not the head of a wild lion but that of her own son.

Had the people of Thebes not refused to dance the Lesser Dance of Dionysos, they would have been saved from the Greater Dance: madness.

The exploration of myths and fairy tales is such a 'lesser dance'. It is a playful descent into an inner world where yet undiscovered potentials — the still uninvited gods and goddesses — are awaiting their redemption. It is a direct encounter with the creative images of the soul.

Chapter 1
Myths and Fairy Tales

Since ancient times, people have told each other stories. As these stories gave expression to fundamental issues, they were passed from generation to generation. Images from myths and fairy tales can convey an ancient knowledge about human experience. They express our deepest longings and fears, and tell of the great questions and problems that people encounter in the course of their lives.

The language of these images is familiar to us. It is a language that the soul itself understands. As mythic images can be experienced, they are a direct access to the deeper levels of ourselves. Unfortunately we have increasingly replaced such images with abstract terms and explanations. As Robert Graves writes in *The White Goddess*:

> 'Nowadays is a civilization in which the prime emblems of poetry are dishonored. In which serpent, lion and eagle belong to the circus-tent; ox, salmon and boar to the cannery; race-horse and greyhound to the betting ring; and the sacred grove to the saw-mill ...'

Instead of experiencing the images of the soul, we now try to explain them from an inner distance. In this way, we have tamed the gods and demons of the soul, but, at the same time, we are in danger of an inner impoverishment and of losing the creative force of our images.

We can now explain what panic is, but Pan, the flute-playing god of the wilderness and the forests, is no longer known to us. We understand eroticism, but the God Eros, son of Aphrodite, we can only meet beyond all understanding in direct experience. Here the music of Pan's flute is familiar to us and we can feel the arrows of Eros, soaked with passion.

Modern psychology speaks a language that cannot be experienced. In abstract terms we try to capture the flow of life. We attempt to understand ourselves as subjects in an objective manner, building up a world of explanations but eventually realizing that the flow of life evades this abstract construction. Alan Watts has described this process as the attempt to pack a parcel with water. Life — like water — is in constant flow. It cannot be wrapped into fixed terms and mechanical laws. Fortunately, the soul flows beyond the limitations of abstract terms and theories as life realizes itself — unstoppable. In an artificial order of statistical norms and laws, we see the soul as a deviation now from what we believe we have wrapped so well.

The attempt to channel the diversity of the soul into generally accepted courses is well established. Modern science is following the Judaeo-Christian tradition in which there was only one god, only one way, and where the original plurality of the gods had to be either integrated or fought against. Today we continue this monotheistic tradition in the form of psychological models which worship an all-powerful ego that knows how to control the many impulses and images, an ego that can dry up the swamps of the soul and conforms to the norms of a technological world.

These inner swamps are, however, inhabited by gods, fairies and trolls who love, dance and sing, and refuse obedience to the guardians of the one god. To the church, this rich diversity was a threat, and in the fourth century, at the Council of Nizea, it was decided to stop the polytheism of the soul. From then on, the creation of religious images was no longer left to the free imagination of the artist, but had to conform to the guidelines of the church.

The images and old customs which did not fit these rulings were in consequence banned from consciousness.

They afterwards lived on the fringes of individual and social life, where the arm of the church could not reach: in dreams, in myths and fairy tales, and sometimes in children's nursery rhymes.

Myths and fairy tales tell of a world with many gods. These gods were an important part of life, and their rich diversity can still be seen today in the ruins of the temples of antiquity. In these places of worship they were honored, and sometimes they travelled through the land. They were colourful in their nature; sometimes graceful, sometimes foolish and at times also cruel and strong. In their many forms, they brought life to the souls of human beings.

Human crises, illnesses and problems were seen as a loss of unity with these gods who worked within people as well as in their environment. In order to return to harmony with a god, people undertook great journeys to the temples where they were reunited with their gods. To be healed, the people opened up to the qualities of their gods. In the Temple of Apollo, they experienced and celebrated the force of the sun within themselves. They became conscious of their inner order. In the Temple of Aphrodite, people responded to feminine forces. They searched for and celebrated the goddess within themselves. In the Temple of Dionysos, they probably danced to unite in ecstasy with their god. They celebrated the forces which thrust them from chaos into creation.

People often spent the night in a temple, cared for by temple servants. With the help of a priest or priestess (and sometimes with hallucinogenic plants) they would listen to the gods and see them in their dreams — as revelations of a hidden dimension which could make a person whole.

Modern psychology — especially where it operates within a medical model — has little space for such revelations. The gods have been replaced by explanations, and so we seek to comply with accepted norms instead of unity with the gods. With the gods, who were vivid and vital, people were able to enter into a lively exchange.

Their crises could become initiation.

Conforming with an understanding of normality that is based on statistics, is very different from a path of initiation. Being 'normal' often means banning these 'gods', our visions and dreams and the qualities that seek to be realized, from our consciousness, or submitting them to the tyranny of an ego that seeks to meet the demands of a standardized world. Where the soul could blossom we too often decide to conform with a vague concept of normality. We are ready to disempower our 'gods' by explanation and then to dismiss them as meaningless in the face of normality.

Once we have distanced ourselves from these 'gods' as the elementary forces of the soul, personal problems lose their deeper meaning. They become a technical problem and are seen as a breakdown of our normal functioning, an inability to conform with the ruling norms.

In myths and legends, crises are always full of meaning. They show the individual in a meaningful and sometimes mysterious exchange with the world from which he is not separate. The human crisis is also the world's crisis, each is related to the other, and both are aspects of the same thing.

This knowledge about our inter-relatedness has been partly lost today. A purely mechanistic scientific thinking regards man as isolated from his environment, as a totally separate unit, 'a sack of skin' (Alan Watts), filled with flesh, bone and a modicum of soul and spirit, but without the diverse, vibrating field of living interrelation through which we have a part in everything that is.

Man, who in his consciousness has separated himself from the meaningful whole, who regards nature as something that is separate from him, has now become its master. He makes the earth subject to him. Nature is being destroyed, and he allows it.

Originally this separation of man and nature, of inner and outer worlds, may have freed human beings from an unconscious symbiosis with nature. It has enabled the awareness of 'I AM'. But, at the same time, is has led to a crisis of proportions we can hardly comprehend. Deluded by the possibilities of modern technology, we have destroyed the natural balance of nature of which we are a part. We have exploited nature thoughtlessly for our short-term goals, and are in the process of poisoning the earth and robbing her of all resources. We have polluted the air that we breathe and the water that we drink. We have extinguished plants and animals and turned parts of our world into concrete deserts in whose waste we are likely to suffocate. We have separated ourselves from harmony with nature and our power is now turning against us.

As a consequence, our behaviour is comparable to that of a cancer cell which spreads rapidly through the body. As the cancer cell is not in harmony with the organism of which it is a part, it destroys the natural balance and becomes a threat to life. The loss of harmony with nature in the outer world is then reflected in the loss of harmony with nature in the inner world. Both are an expression of the same crisis.

As long as we do not recognize this connection between inner and outer worlds, the environmental crises and the problems inside us, our illnesses and emotional and spiritual conflicts appear as isolated phenomena which strike in a meaningless way. But we have now reached a point where through technology the crisis can no longer be ignored, and where each further interference is causing more damage.

At this crucial point, we have to ask about the meaning of our crises. To solve our problems, we have to come to a wholistic understanding of ourselves and realize that we are a part of a much larger organism. We are supported in this by the perception of modern physics which has come to see this separation of man and nature, of inner and outer worlds as a misunderstanding beyond which new horizons are opening. We can also learn from the wisdom of native people who have never questioned their inter-relatedness with nature. Finally, we can also remember an ancient esoteric understanding of the oneness of all life which is still existent in our culture. This understanding we find in myths and fairy tales.

The Grail Legend provides a powerful image of this relation between the inner and outer worlds. There is the old Grail King, who was wounded in the regenerative organs by a spear. He is in agony, and his wounds will not heal. And at the same time, the rivers are no longer flowing, the springs have dried up, the land has turned to desert. As the legend shows, his suffering is an inner correspondent with the starving of his land. Both are an expression of the same crisis of life.

In our consciousness, we have separated ourselves from the world. In doing so we have broken away from a meaningful context, and more and more people are now feeling lonely, and regard their lives as empty and devoid of meaning. This feeling of emptiness might lead many people to a host of doctors and psychologists who, as long as they regard a person as an entity that is separate from his environment, cannot effect real healing. Even more refined technologies and psychological techniques cannot help, as long as their goal is the taming and control of our inner nature. On the contrary, if we continue to measure a person by questionable criteria (such as 'ill' or 'normal'), or pin him down clinically where it is a question of freeing yet unlived potentials, we are preventing the necessary breakthrough to a new consciousness.

In other words: in psychology we should finally abandon belief in technology and begin to recognize the deeper meaning in our crises. We should seek to reinstate harmony with the forces of nature within us — and in the world of which we are a part. Psychology does not need to become more sophisticated in its techniques: it needs to change its fundamental orientation. Only then can the therapy of the soul become an ecology of life where inner and outer worlds become one.

Parzival's journey, as described in the Grail Legend, is a search for harmony with the forces of life. His journey is fascinating today, because Parzifal was prepared to go beyond the rigid limitations of his time. At the beginning of his journey, Parzifal is the 'pure fool', who — like the youngest brother in fairy tales — is ridiculed, but as he is not restrained by the prevalent beliefs and does not even know what normality means, is able to listen with an open heart. In this way he can perceive and realize the extraordinary.

Today Parzival might be in danger of getting caught up in a net of therapeutic approaches. Possibly he would work on his dependency on his mother, and raise his confidence to assert himself against the sorceress Cundry's accusations. Perhaps he would also succeed in freeing himself from his compulsive attraction to the Grail in order to pursue a career as a knight, or enter the church. Just as Freud reduced Moses to a pathological case, so it would be possible to diagnose Parzival as sick, and in need of appropriate therapy. What would remain beyond such a diagnosis would be an impoverished existence — a person robbed of his individual meaning, who is struck by meaningless symptoms — a victim.

The role of the victim is very popular today. As a victim, a person suffers under the burden of his crises and problems. As he does not feel responsible for his conflicts, he is not able to solve them either. Unable to sense any meaning in his crisis, he feels weak and empty.

Myths and fairy tales can show a different perspective. In myths, the crisis is always full of meaning — it is an important part of the story. Without crises, there would be no myths or legends. Crisis is the pathos in Greek tragedy, a conflict with the gods or the expulsion from paradise. In it, our own problems and difficulties are mirrored as a call to consciousness. It is the challenge to restore harmony with the forces of one's being. It is a 'sacred wound', a call, through which a person enters on a journey. By accepting this challenge, he can transform his crisis into an heroic journey.

Chapter 2
The Hero's Journey

Myths and fairy tales tell the story of a hero's journey. Although these tales originate from very different times and cultures and accordingly are very diverse in their images, it seems as if there is a common pattern underlying them. Joseph Campbell has written extensively about this pattern. He has shown how it corresponds to the mysteries and initiation rites of ancient cultures out of which, in the course of time, myths and legends have come to be.

As a mythological pattern the Hero's Journey is a conceptual model, a map enabling us to grasp our own experiences as part of a significant process of personal unfolding. It is a basic pattern of human development

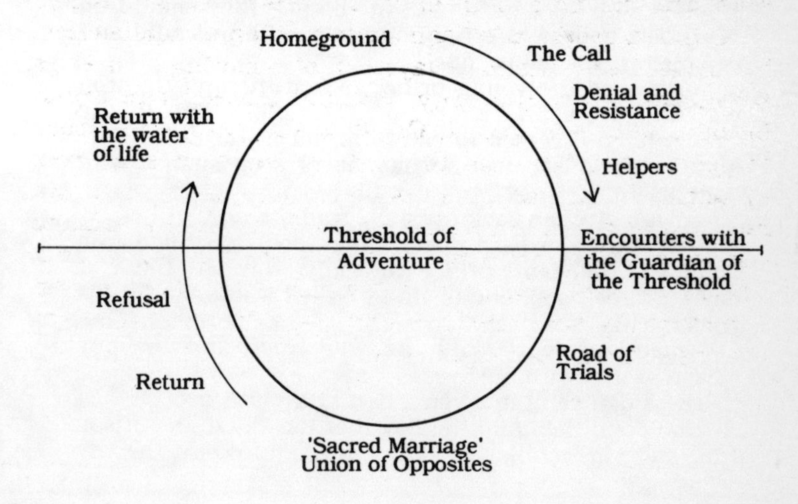

which allows us to see inner and outer changes in our lives within a meaningful context. The pattern of the Hero's Journey can mirror our own conflicts and illnesses but also our creative breakthroughs and the necessary descents into an inner underworld, in the process of psychotherapy.

We can imagine the journey of the hero as a spiral. The hero can be a man or a woman; in myths and fairy tales it is sometimes a god, a mystic being or an animal. The journey can be an adventure — often it is a journey inwards. Uusually it begins with a familiar situation, the homeground. In the Grimms' tale of Iron John this homeground is a castle garden, and it is here where the hero hears a call to adventure:

> The king had gone hunting and the little prince was playing with a golden ball, when suddenly something happened that was to change his life: the golden ball slipped out of his hand and rolled into the cage where the king kept a wild man prisoner. (Formerly, this wild man had lived in a magic forest from which many people had vanished without trace: one day, when a hunter was riding into the forest, he saw a giant hairy arm rise out of a pond and pull down his dog into the depth of the water. When the king heard this he ordered the pond to be emptied with buckets, and at the bottom they found Iron John. His body was strong and hairy, he was wild and completely covered in mud.)
>
> Wide-eyed the young prince looked through the iron bars into Iron John's prison. The golden ball in the giant's hands seemed to call him, but at the same time he was afraid because he had never seen such a wild man before.
>
> 'Please give me back my ball,' said the boy.
>
> 'Not until you have opened the door', answered Iron John, and the young prince ran sadly away. But the next day he came back, and again he asked Iron John for his golden ball.
>
> 'Open my door', said the wild man, and the boy looked at him with big eyes.
>
> He said, 'I can't free you, I don't have the key.'
>
> Iron John then told the boy that the key to the prison was under his mother's pillow. On the third day, the boy

returned — with the key. He wanted to have his golden ball back and so he forgot about everything else. As he opened the heavy iron gate he injured his finger. The wild man, however, gave him back his ball and ran off into the forest.

'Please don't run away,' cried the prince. 'My parents will beat me when they discover I have freed you!'

The giant came back once again, lifted the boy onto his shoulders and ran away with him.

For the prince, the golden ball in the hands of Iron John was a call to adventure. As the golden ball slipped out of his hands and rolled into the cage, a part of him moved from the world of a child into an area where a hairy giant — his own masculinity — was waiting for him. Watching the wild man through the iron bars, the boy had come to the threshold linking childhood to manhood. He had lost his toy, and the forces of his own wild masculinity began to call. He had to get hold of the key to this new world, which lay hidden under his mother's pillow, in order to open the iron gate — the entrance to his own manhood. In doing so, he followed his own call and began a journey which the fairy tale describes in detail. Initially, the boy had to guard the golden well of Iron John, and then he had to go through several trials, As an unknown knight on one of Iron John's horses, he eventually frees a foreign kingdom and marries the daughter of the king.

The call is the beginning of a journey. It often reaches a person on the edge of a familiar life situation, where he might be unexpectedly touched by signs or encounters of a so-far unknown and hidden world. In myths and fairy tales this often happens at a deep well or at the edge of a dark forest, or under an old tree. The messengers of the call are sometimes animals which speak with human voices: a frog, as he appears in the tale of the Frog Prince; or a fish that appears from the depth of the ocean, as in the tale of the Fisher and his Wife. They represent a symbolic connection with the unconscious and the world of instinct.

Sometimes the messengers of the call are mysterious strangers in whose being we feel the magic of an unknown world. Such are the knights that Parzifal meets in the forest of Soltane, and whom he takes to be gods because their armour is more beautiful than anything he has ever seen. In everyday consciousness such figures may seem strange at first. On a deeper level, however, these messengers of future experiences might already be familiar. It seems as if they are an embodiment of a deep longing.

In our own lives the call can reach us in many ways. It may enter our lives through a friend who tells us of fantastic experiences and events in a world that we do not yet know. But suddenly we feel affected, we listen and may feel that we are approaching an essential part of ourselves. Like the young prince, we find ourselves then at the threshold of a new world.

At every moment, a call can meet us. Suddenly we are totally connected to ourselves and feel what is really important to us. It might arrive when a friend tells us of experiences in Asia, or when we are alone on a rock far above the sea, listening to the rhythms of the waves, or on a peak of a mountain, or under a tree through which an autumn storm is raging. Suddenly we feel something essential. A call can also reach us through the intensity of a personal relationship, or reveal itself in the images of our dreams, or through an illness in which our view becomes focused on the essential.

The experience of a call is different for each person. What touches one can leave another entirely indifferent: whereas Parzifal, when he encountered the knights of King Arthur's Round Table, felt his call as a burning desire, the Little Mermaid may have disappeared laughing and unconcerned from the rocks into the waves.

It is a call to departure. It reminds us to realize the things that are essential in our lives. And often it throws us into an inner crisis: on the one hand we are ready to leave right away, but at the same time we begin to see the many reasons why we cannot go — maybe we have professional obligations, a family, a house, and more. The denial and the resistance to the call are important steps in the journey of the hero. They demand an inner decision. In this conflict between that which calls us and that which holds us, our view is directed inwards. Here we might encounter images and dreams of our childhood, or feelings that we have not so far experienced. To make the journey our own, we have to look inwards and make a conscious decision.

It is a difficult task to follow one's inner calling. As long as there is the possibility of avoiding it, a person might refuse to go. But even if he continued to live as if nothing had happened, it is as if his spiritual and emotional centre of gravity has already moved into a new world. A chain of signs and experiences keep reminding him, until one day the hero goes on his way. It is only then that a person comes in contact again with his own centre.

If a person refuses to listen to this inner calling which gives meaning to life, the denial can lead to illness. The illness itself is then a part of the inner struggle, an urgent reminder to follow one's call.

Rolling Thunder, an American Indian Shaman, asks a patient during a healing ritual why he wants to get well. He asks him about the qualities that call him, because if a person is in touch with his inner calling, if he lives his inner vocation, he has access to great sources of strength, through which even serious illnesses can be healed.

Once the hero sets out on the journey, he finds access to forces that strengthen him. In myths and fairy tales, he meets the helpers on the edge of the road. Sometimes these are tiny old ladies or animals who can give valuable advice to the hero, or maybe a magical ring which will protect him on his journey. In some tales the helper is a ferryman who will carry the hero across the water. In our daily lives, this helper might be a friend or a relative, or sometimes even a therapist who is able to recognize our conflict and can encourage us to go our own way. Such people reinforce the hero to leave behind the familiar world and to enter into an unknown realm of adventure that is beyond our conscious control.

In the world of myths and fairy tales, there are sometimes mysterious or dangerous beings who live beyond the boundaries of the village. They might be gnomes and elves, or giants and ogres whose ugliness repels us. Those beings are often the guardians of the threshold to a hidden world. It is at this threshold where we also find the god Pan, who plays the flute for the magical round dances of the Nymphs. And it is here that people might experience the panic, the sudden and apparently unfounded horror, that Pan imposes on mortals once they cross the threshold and enter into his realm. In many stories this is the place where the hero has to enter into a battle with a guardian of the threshold.

In astrology, the axis from the ascendant to the descendant separates the zodiac and the circle of the houses in an upper (outer) and a lower (inner) world. In a similar way, the threshold of adventure is the access to the realm of the soul. Over this threshold the hero is led through mysterious tests and adventures, to his innermost destination, like Odysseus on his journeys or Parzival in his search for the Grail.

The fairy tale of Mother Holle gives a graphic illustration of this threshold:

> A young girl whose mother had died had to sit daily on the street and spin beside a well. The girl spun every day until her fingers began to bleed. Once, as she washed the blood from her fingers, the spindle fell into the well and disappeared. The girl cried and told her stepmother of her misfortune, but her stepmother scolded her and said hard-heartedly: 'If you let the spindle fall into the well, then you must go and get it out again!' The girl returned to the well and did not know what to do. To find the spindle again, she jumped into the well where she lost consciousness. When she awoke, she found herself in a beautiful meadow full of flowers under the shining sun.

By her jump into the well, the girl had crossed the threshold of adventure. To do this, she had to become dead to the normal world — by giving up every familiar thing — and jump into a deep well. On the other side, however, was the realm of Mother Holle, Germanic Goddess of Fertility. Here the girl awakened to new life.

> She now found herself on a road of trials: from a baker's oven the loaves cried out, 'Oh, pull us out, pull us out, or we will burn!'. And a tree full of apples cried, 'Oh, shake us, shake us, we apples are all ripe!'. The girls took the bread from the oven and shook the apples from the tree. At last, she met Mother Holle, and in her service she shook out the feather beds so that it was snowing on the earth. When spring came, the girl returned covered with gold to the earth.

This journey into the underworld of which many myths and fairy tales speak, follows in its structure shamanistic initiation rituals from many cultures. We will discuss such rituals in more detail in the context of the Grail legend.

Across the threshold the hero enters on the road of trials, and eventually reaches the lowest point of the cycle. Here he is 'healed'. He becomes one with the qualities that first called him. In the language of alchemy, this is the 'Sacred Marriage' where the opposites become one. This often happens in an ecstatic act. Through this process of becoming whole, the hero is initiated into a new dimension of his being. He becomes a master of many worlds which are now no longer separated. Like the Shaman who lives and works in the reality of his village but is also rooted in the spiritual world, the hero can now reach beyond his original limitations. He has become one with the forces of his being.

Enlightened and enriched, the hero then returns. Often this is a new challenge. The hero now has to carry 'the water of life' back into society. He has to realize his experiences in the world. Here, too, there is often a refusal to leave the state of ecstasy and happiness in order to return to the profane world. Those who know the state of unity, know how hard it is to leave it. However, only with the return to the world is the hero's journey complete. The hero needs the community to anchor his experiences, and the community needs the renewal from this experience of another world which justifies the long absence of the hero.

Once the hero crosses the threshold again, he has to

leave behind his helpers and their magic objects. Changed from within, he returns into his community. In rituals of initiation, this return is often celebrated as a new birth, from where further cycles can unfold.

The hero's journey is a pattern of completely-lived experience. It is a map that offers orientation in times of change. During crises or illness, this map can prepare us for the necessary descent into an inner world. It can help to recognize one's own call, but also to understand that denial is an important part of the journey. With the help of this map, we can understand and accept our conflicts as a creative and meaningful process. On this journey, a person is not a victim burdened with neuroses, illnesses and impossible trouble, but a hero in search of his own destiny.

In earlier times, this descent into an underworld was celebrated in our own rituals and festivals. Many such rituals are lost today. To some extent, we can still find them in churches, and also in the padded rooms of psychotherapists or of therapy centres.

Without such a ritual framework in which we can live through changes in a conscious way, it is difficult to go with the flow of life and allow for changes. When change is called for, we often hold back. It frightens us when someone leaves the realm that we consider normal and healthy. It is difficult to follow our own calling, and often we prefer to live unnoticed outside ourselves. The return from a world beyond the ordinary into society is also difficult for us. Instead of returning the water of life back to society, we often prefer to retreat to a spiritual or therapeutic island. Our journey thus remains incomplete.

In the old customs and rituals these cycles could be experienced in their totality. In the absence of such a ritual framework, myths and fairy tales play a very important role. As their images come to life in us, we are able to follow the paths of initiation of their heroes. Through stories, we can experience all of the cycles of life. Myths are thus a living access to initiation.

Chapter 3
The Dance with the Gods

In antiquity, people united with their gods in the temples. These temples were decorated with pictures and statues through which people could experience the mythological being of a god. The many gods and goddesses correspond to a great diversity within the human soul. Through ritual unification with these gods, people aroused corresponding qualities in their own being. To worship the gods was to celebrate the forces of life within.

Today, as the temples in the outer world are no longer operating, our body can become a temple where we can celebrate the diverse forces within ourselves. Through our bodies we can experience the power of our images and awaken in ourselves the forces of life. To experience images in our body is to leave behind the role of observer. Our images can move us, and if we follow this movement we are already in a 'sacred dance' as it has been danced since ancient times.

Dance is the most direct form of expression. To many native people, it is a direct access to the gods. The Australian Aborigines, for example, enter the Dreamtime in dance: this is the time in which the gods have lived and still live, in which they have created the world and still continue to do so. Through their dance, this Dreamtime becomes present. In dance they experience the power of the spirit ancestors, Alcheringa and Tjukurpa. In their movements they re-enact the deeds of their gods of which myths from the Dreamtime tell.

These myths are images of creation, telling of giant

Australian Aborigines in dance to evoke the Spirits (from C.A. Burland: Mythos of Life and Death, *Rugby, Jolly & Barber, 1974).*

serpents that found their way from the centre of the earth to its surface, thereby creating mountains, valleys and ravines. They tell of beings that came from the skies and the oceans; they awaken images from the birth of water and fire, and show how the first whale found its way to the coast of Australia. As people allow themselves to be moved by these images, they experience the Dreamtime in the present. This dance is complete surrender. its goal is to become one with the power; it is an ecstatic act.

As we allow ourselves to follow our images with our bodies, so we can return to this most original form of dance. Children are masters in this art of unconditional surrender. Through imitation, they completely surrender themselves to images from their imagination. With complete devotion, they transform themselves into a plant, an animal, or an adult. Through imitation they directly experience the beings of their mysterious world.

The art of experiencing the essence of another person within ourselves is of great importance in therapeutic work. To experience another person's special way of being, I have often imitated other people. I have looked for a body posture which corresponded to the person I was dealing with. I tried to breathe in the same way, and imitated their characteristic movements. In this way, I could experience in my own body how a person stood on the earth. I have felt, for example, another person's tense neck or shoulders. Through this process I found a much deeper understanding, and could experience the inner condition from which this person engaged with their world.

In the same way, we can approach the images and forces within ourselves. To invite them as 'gods', we can search for a bodily posture through which an inner image begins to resonate and awakens to life. Through one particular posture, we can experience Pan, the god of the wilderness. In another posture we can feel the power and passion of the Sumerian goddess, Innana. The myths that tell of these gods can serve as access to inner experience.

To find such postures we have to listen inwardly and allow an inner image to emerge. Slowly this image can take shape in the body; we can feel it through slow movements, and accept it with our bodies until the image and its atmosphere finds itself in the posture of our body, where it comes to life.

The point of this game is not an outward performance corresponding to a much later development of dance, but rather to find an inner experience and a congruence between our images and feelings, and the posture of our bodies. In this congruence, our images can awaken in every part of the body. Every image and each emotion can then be embodied in a conscious posture, or a movement of the body, in an expression that matches our inner experience. From this congruence, this being fully where we are, a personal journey can unfold: from here a process can begin. The witch, for example, is thus no longer a frightening figure in the external world, but a force within ourselves, representing what is witchlike in us. As we allow ourselves to be moved by this force, she loses her frightfulness. She becomes an invited goddess: her strength becomes an enrichment to our lives.

As we allow ourselves to move with the many figures from myths and fairy tales, it is possible to experience their powers within ourselves. Once we link these images with a slow flowing movement similar to a Tai Chi movement, we are able to experience the flow of a story in a very direct form — a dance is born. In this dance, we leave the fixation on the boundaries of our 'small ego' and learn the art of transformation. In the flow of movement, new images and feelings can emerge. Perhaps we will discover a joy that we have not yet lived, or the hurt that we have not yet suffered, or an unresolved anger, or pleasures we have so far denied ourselves. Images from our childhood may emerge and sometimes also painful memories. If we have buried the hurt from childhood in a muscular armour, we may feel this hurt now as we allow the tension from our muscles to be released. As in fairy tales, this is the moment of redemption when accumulated tension can be released. Through movement we can allow our images and feelings expression in our bodies — and flow with them.

All experiences are stored in the body, which, moved by mythic images, can then complete its unfinished stories, thus completing the processes we have not yet fully lived. This is an inner dance, a dance of our images, our feelings and visions. 'It is a dance that can carry us far beyond anything that we have ever dreamed ...' — the lesser dance of Dionysos.

This work with myths and fairy tales, which I teach in seminars* in many places, is a means of awakening this 'lesser dance' to life. Myths and fairy tales give direct access to the deeper layers of the human soul. their images are a doorway to the personal and transpersonal — archetypal experiences. To introduce the nature of this work through a living process — not replacing the power of images by abstract explanation — this book follows the thread of a legend. It tells the story of Parzival's search for the Grail.

The Grail Legend is a very powerful story which draws on ancient wisdom from many cultures. The roots of this legend reach back into the mythology of the Celts, but also to the mysticism of early Christianity and the vegetation rituals of the old cultures of Asia. In the Middle Ages it was recorded by Chrestien de Troyes for the Count of Flanders. In his own words, it was the best story ever told in a royal court. Because of the poet's death the legend remained initially incomplete and was continued by many other poets.

In the beginning of the fourteenth century, the story was told in Germany by Wolfram von Eschenbach, in a complete version. Wolfram von Eschenbach was a mystic who knew the esoteric origins of the Grail Legend. His narrative describes a path of initiation. In the steps of this journey we find basic experiences that a person today still encounters on a journey of personal development.

In this book, I will follow the steps of this journey. I will discuss questions and issues that relate to each step and will show possibilities of entering a creative process with the images of a legend. The Grail Legend is an extraordinarily rich story which today seems to touch people in a special way. The central motif of a land that under the dominion of a sick king turned to desert and needs redemption, is a strong image of the problems of our century. Parzival's story describes a personal journey in which a person redeems the ailing king and the desert land. It describes the search for the Grail as a journey to inner wholeness. Through its images, it can lead us to issues and experiences that are still important today on the journey of inner development. I have mentioned some of these issues in the context of the Hero's Journey. Our ancestry and relationship to our own roots is one such issue that is directly connected to the beginning of a personal journey.

* If you wish to receive a programme for these seminars, write to: Transpersonal Psychology Centre
66 Paterson Street
Byron Bay
New South Wales 2481
Australia.

Chapter 4
The Grail Legend

Ancestry

In many myths and legends a hero's journey begins with a narration of his ancestry. Through our ancestors we are directly connected with a particular landscape and the history of a culture. Biologically, but also spiritually and emotionally, the experiences of our ancestors are alive in us. In a sense, our ancestry is thus the ground in which a personal journey is rooted. To the American Indians the access to these roots is a very important experience. Their connection to their ancestors is a source of power. It is a doorway to a sacred knowledge that is entered in rituals. Through this connection their actions are given a meaning which reaches far beyond the limits of an individual's life.

It is difficult in our culture to recognize our ancestry as a part of our own journey. Most of us are not conscious of our ancestors and often we know very little of their lives and their experiences. From an American Indian's point of view, our world picture has become egocentric as we have lost connection with our roots. Our understanding of the questions and problems of life has become ahistoric and self-centred.

The evolution of man is a continuum, however, that starts long before the birth of an individual person and reaches far beyond his death. In this continuum, the biological characteristics and experiences of our ancestors are connected with yet unlived possibilities of human development. In every moment of life, the past — personal and transpersonal history — touches the future. The span of an individual life and the contents of a personal journey are thus embedded in a much larger development, whose reality can be experienced in our relationship with our ancestors.

Often the qualities and experiences that call a person onto a journey are mysteriously connected with their personal and transpersonal history. Many myths and fairy tales thus begin with the story of a hero's ancestors. In Wolfram von Eschenbach's story, Parzival's journey begins long before his birth with the story of his parents. Through this, Parzival's call and his particular journey becomes understandable.

Parzival's father, Gahmuret, was an adventurous knight, as were many at the time of the Crusades. Instead of sharing his inheritance with his brother, Galoes, Gahmuret was drawn into the world. As a knight, he wanted to court women for their favors and increase his fame in battle. With precious materials and jewels and an army of pages, cooks, fiddlers and drummers, Gahmuret left his home country. He wanted to serve none less than the most powerful of all kings, the Caliph of Baghdad. Gahmuret had the reputation of invincible strength. In the service of the Caliph he fought against the Egyptians, and accompanied by victories he travelled through many countries of the East.

In Africa, a storm drove Gahmuret into the port of the city of Patelamunt. This was the kingdom of a black queen, Belakane. Her city was under siege from a hostile army. Gahmuret conquered her enemies. He freed the city from its siege, and when he married the black queen became Emperor of the land of Sarazenes. Gahmuret was happy with Belakane, but soon became restless again. His heart longed for new adventures. Although he loved the queen dearly (and she was expecting his child) he left her one night and returned by ship to Europe.

Gahmuret was a person who was always driven. At the beginning of his journey, he had a panther in his coat of arms, but now he carried the image of an anchor on his shield. The panther was an expression of his great strength and his search for something higher which drove him through many culture of the East. The image of the anchor reveals his longing for inner depth and a foundation to give him stability.

In Europe, Gahmuret went to his cousin, Kaylet, in Toledo. Here he came to know of a great tournament where the best knights of all Europe would gather. The queen, Herzeloyde, had promised to marry the knight who would emerge as a victor from the battle. Gahmuret went immediately on his way. As King of Zazamanc, with great pomp, trumpets, drums and flutes, he entered the town of Kanvoleis. The queen was embarrassed by his appearance, but in the battle Gahmuret conquered all the other knights.

Later, when the queen greeted him in the palace, he was deeply touched, but his restless heart did not want to settle down, it called for new adventures. Gahmuret told the queen of his journeys through the East and his relationship with Belakane, and he asked her to let him go again. But during the conversation, Herzeloyde became fond of the young knight. She asked him to stay with her, and she promised him the freedom to take part in knightly adventures whenever he wished. At the same time, she asked him to return to her when he had completed his adventures.

A big wedding was now celebrated in Kanvoleis and a happy year began for Gahmuret and Herzeloyde. It almost seemed as if Gahmuret had found peace and inner depth, when a call from the Caliph reached him for help in a decisive battle against the Babylonians. Gahmuret did not want to go. He was happy with Herzeloyde, who was expecting a child, but in his heart he could not refuse the call to new adventure. Again he left the queen, and through betrayal he lost his life in a battle. Even before a faithful servant broke the news of his death, the queen anticipated the tragedy. She had a strange dream. She felt carried through the air by a meteor. All around her, lightning was flashing, thunder rolled and fiery tears rained down upon her. A big bird was tearing at her right hand. It seemed as if she was the nurse of a terrible dragon who tore her heart from her chest, sucked on her breast and flew quickly away.

When the queen awoke, a servant brought the spear-head which had killed Gahmuret, and the shirt he had worn in his last battle. The queen fell into deep sadness. She felt a stinging pain in her body and fell unconscious to the floor. Fourteen days later, she gave birth to a boy, whom she named Parzival. Although Gahmuret's death caused the queen great despair, she also felt some happiness: in Parzival she recognized the traits of her beloved husband, and it seemed to her that she had once more taken Gahmuret into her arms.

These were the circumstances into which Parzival was born. It is the moment in astrology when a horoscope is made. Like a seed that contains the life-forces of a plant, the quality of this moment in time contains something of the forces that will become a part of Parzival's journey. In a seminar we once explored the qualities of this moment through movement. You can discover this experience for yourself through the following guided journey.

Guided Journeys are journeys of inner exploration. They are a vital access to your own images and experiences. You can undertake such journeys in your imagination — as a dance of your images — or through movement of your body. The images of such journeys are already alive in you, but often they are unfocused, as in a dream. In Guided Journeys it is possible to unleash the power of these images and experience them with full awareness.

To explore your own images it is useful to close your eyes. When your view is no longer directed outward, you can begin to look inward. It is useful to be accompanied by a friend or partner. He or she can read to you the text of a Guided Journey slowly and with pauses. After the journey you can talk with your partner about your experiences, and if you wish you can then change roles. If you go on these journeys alone, you can record them onto a cassette. In this way, too, your focus will be directed inward.

Possibly you might just want to read these journeys and absorb them like a story, discovering deeper dimensions of the Grail Legend and encountering images and experiences of your own life journey.

Through the following Guided Journey you will be able to experience the qualities of the moment into which you were born. Beyond words and explanations, you can discover a direct understanding of your origins and the beginning of your own journey.

Close your eyes and focus your attention inward. Let your breathing flow gently, and relax. In your mind's eye let the images of the Grail Legend emerge. Parzival's journey begins with the union of Gahmuret and Herzeloyde.

The Father

Gahmuret is a knight who is always called by new adventures. He is a fighter and his search for depth and a stable background remains unfulfilled. In his coat of arms is a panther, ready to jump, and also an anchor, searching for land.

Find a bodily posture that expresses Gahmuret's being. Let this image of Gahmuret move in every part of your body. Give it expression with the posture of your back, with your hands and legs. Feel this knight in your breathing, in the way you hold your head and the expression of your face. Thus you can experience in your own body Gahmuret's great strength and the qualities of his being.

The Mother

Wolfram describes Herzeloyde as a woman of great purity. She is a beautiful woman, she is delicate, and she loves Gahmuret with all her heart. Her suffering reveals a great depth.

Let this image of Herzeloyde come alive as well. Give it expression in every part of your body and in your breathing. Find a posture for Herzeloyde that allows you to experience the purity and the depth of her feminine being.

Both of these body postures embody a world of particular experiences. Let yourself connect these two postures now in a flowing movement. Let them enter into relation as you slowly move back and forth between these two postures in your body. In this movement you can discover something of the quality of the relation between Gahmuret and Herzeloyde. It is from this relation that Parzival came to be.

Let your movements become stronger now. Give them force and intensity and surrender to the flow of your movements.

The Child

When your movements become slower again, a new posture can develop: the child. Let the image of this child awaken in your body as well.

At the beginning of your own life journey, too, was the relationship of your parents. In movement — or in the imagination of your body movements — you can explore the interplay of qualities in this relation.

Become aware of your father's way of being, and in your mind's eye find an image of your own father. In what surroundings do you find your father? What kind of clothes is he wearing? Possibly you can imagine a coat of arms, or an animal that corresponds to your father's way of being. Look inward, and give your images expression in your body. Explore these images in the posture of your body, in the expression of your face, in the way you hold your hands, in your legs, your back and the way you breath and move. Find a posture in which you can feel the image of your father in your own body.

Now let an image of your mother appear in your mind's eye. Where do you see her? What clothes does she wear? What is the atmosphere that surrounds her? Again you might find a symbol or an animal which is related to the essence of your own mother. Let an image emerge, and give it expression with your whole body. Find a posture in which you can experience the essence of your mother in your own body.

In a slow movement you can now connect these two postures. As you flow back and forth between the image of your mother and that of your father, you can explore the specific qualities in the relationship between your parents. It is from this relationship that you have come to be.

Let your movements become stronger now. Give them power and intensity and surrender to the flow of your images. Let a dance begin ... When your movements become slower again, you can find a new posture in your body: the child. It is the child you once were, and which is still alive in you. Let this child express itself in your body now, let it come alive ...

The connection to our parents gives direct access to our own roots. Initially, you may find it difficult to feel the qualities of your father and mother in your own body (and sometimes these qualities might be the last thing you would like to find within yourself). The power of our ancestors is a part of us, however. We have come into being from their cells, and their characteristic features are alive in us as well. If we become aware of these qualities they will not rule our lives but enrich our ways of being. As we accept the qualities of our ancestors we become able to grow beyond their limitations.

If we find it difficult to feel the child within ourselves, we may become aware that we have lost touch with that vital part of ourselves. Closed doors, too, can help us to find a way in the right direction. They can make us reflect and search for ways to invite into our lives the qualities we are not yet living. The experience of difficulties can thus become a bridge to new ways of being.

Chapter 5
The Call

With the child in her arms and accompanied by a handful of servants, Herzeloyde moved to a farmhouse in the solitude of Soltane. Gahmuret's death had struck her deeply. Parzival should never learn of the world of knighthood. She made all the servants promise never to speak of the world of knights or of Parzival's father. Far away from the world of the courts, in the isolation of the forests, she wanted to raise Parzival, and she hoped he would never leave her.

Parzival was a wild child. He had a strong will and extraordinary depth of feeling. With bow and arrow he moved through the forests, but if he hit a bird he would break into tears of compassion. In the solitude of the forests his life was totally rooted in nature. He did not know that beyond the forests there was another world, but sometimes, when he listened to the song of the birds, he was touched by a deep longing and in tears would run to his mother. It was this longing that his mother feared. To protect the boy she ordered all birds of the forests to be caught and killed, but when Parzival came to the scene he was outraged and set the birds free again. His mother told him now about God who had created all beings, and also about the Devil who ruled over the forces of darkness.

Untroubled but with uncertain longings, Parzival roamed through the forests of Soltane, and here, in the solitude, he was reached by a call. One day he heard a strange noise. Five armed knights were galloping on their horses through the forest. Branches were crashing against their heavy armour and their iron shirts. The boy could hear but could not see them, as they came towards him at a walk. He was filled with awe, and said:

> 'By my soul, my lady my mother's words were true when she told me that devils are the foulest thing in the world; she taught me that to counter them a man should always cross himself; but I shall spurn that advice! I'm not going to cross myself — no, I'm going to strike the very strongest with one of my javelins; for then, I think, none of the others will dare come near me.'

So said the boy to himself before he saw the knights; but when he saw them openly, no longer hidden by the trees, and saw their hauberks shimmering, their helmets burnished and dazzling, saw the white and the red shining brightly in the sun, and the gold and blue and silver, he thought them glorious indeed, and cried:

> 'Oh thank you God! These are angels I see here! And truly, I have sinned terribly and done great wrong, saying that they were devils. My mother told me no fable when she said that angels were the fairest things there are, under God, whose beauty surpasses all other. But now, I think, I see God himself! For I can see one so fair that, God defend me, the others seem not one tenth as beautiful. My mother told me that we should worship God above all things and pray to Him and honor Him, and I shall worship that one there and all the angels after Him.'
>
> (After Chrestien de Troyes, *Perceval)*

Parzival went down on his knees. Again and again he called out, 'Help me, merciful God! Help me God, only you can bring mercy.' The knights watched the strange boy with great surprise. The sovereign explained that he was not God, but that he hoped to serve God as a knight. Parzival then examined the armor of the knights with fascination. They seemed more beautiful to him than anything he had ever seen:

> 'What is a knight?' he asked, as he examined the sword of the sovereign. 'If you are not God, then tell me, how do you become a knight?'

'King Arthur can make you a knight,' the sovereign answered. 'If you go to his court, he will make you a knight. It seems as if you too are of knightly descent.'

When Parzival returned to his mother he told her of his encounter: 'Mother, I have seen five men who were more beautiful than God. They told me of knighthood and of King Arthur who will make me a knight!'

Herzeloyde felt that she could no longer hold him back. Unconscious, she fell to the ground.

After Wolfram von Eschenbach, *Parzival.*

The encounter with the knights had touched a force in Parzival which now needed to be realized. To follow this call he had to cross the boundaries of his mother's world.

The call is the soul's longing for itself. If a person does not hear this calling from within, he will miss a dimension of experience that gives meaning to life. If he follows his inner calling, however, a hero's journey can unfold which can guide him through many adventures towards his own destination.

In Egypt it was told that each person has come from a star into the world to fulfil a specific task upon the earth. When a person is born into the world, however, he forgets his star and also his task. In the course of his life he might then perhaps encounter a person or a situation which will awaken the memory of his star. Suddenly he knows why he is on earth, and may feel a strong sense of his own destiny.

The encounter with the knights awakens this sense of destiny in Parzival. The sovereign, too, seems to recognize Parzival's inner destination. In spite of his foolish appearance he recognizes his knightly descent; he becomes a helper who points the way into the world of knights.

In the following Guided Journey you can awaken the experience of your own calling. This journey into your imagination has three parts: the first part will lead you into the world of your own images; in the second part your actual journey will begin (in this part it is best to be accompanied by some music, some suggestions for which can be found at the end of the book). If you undertake this journey together with a partner you can tell him/her in this part about your image and experiences, as if you were telling a story. As you tell a partner about your images or sensations your own experience will deepen and become clearer. In the third part of the journey you will meet an ally. In silence (without communicating with your partner) you can enter into a dialogue with a helper.

Lie down on a flat surface and make yourself comfortable. To focus your attention inward, close your eyes and cover them with a cloth. Let your breath flow gently and begin to relax your whole body. Let all tension flow from your muscles and feel yourself being carried by the earth. When you feel quiet and relaxed your journey begins ...

Imagine that you are standing at a deep well surrounded by large old trees. The rocks of this well are ancient, they are covered with moss. You can hear the wind in the trees, and with your hands you can feel the pleasant coolness of the rocks at the edge of the well. As you bend forward and look into the well, you can see your own reflection in the depth of the water. At first your image is clear — and then it begins to change, showing your different parts of yourself.

On the surface of the water you can now see the image of a child. If is the child you once were ...

As the wind blows, a leaf falls in to the well. The water begins to move — and your image disappears. When the water becomes calm again, you see another image of yourself. You can see yourself in a moment when you were very happy, a time and place where you really felt your own essence and your life force. As you look at this image you can see in the depth of the water the atmosphere and the feelings of this special moment.

The wind in the trees is blowing more strongly now, and as the surface of the water begins to move your image disappears. In the depth of the well you can now recognize the image of a path, which leads across a meadow to a large doorway. Imagine that you enter this image. You are walking along the path. You can feel the ground beneath your feet, the sun is shining and you might smell the scents of grasses and herbs. You continue to follow this path, and, dreamlike, you find yourself in front of this large, ancient doorway. Let yourself explore it.

On the other side of the doorway is a world of images and experiences that are directly related to your own calling. It is a realm in which all dreams can come true and where everything is possible. As you explore this ancient doorway, you realize that it is unlocked. Slowly, you open the door, and enter into a world of your dreams and visions, following your images and the impulses of your body.

At this point the music can begin. If you make this journey with a partner you can now tell him or her of your images and experiences as they unfold. Your partner will listen to you, but he/she must not answer or engage in a conversation. He/she must be present and encourage you to speak as your images unfold.

After ten or fifteen minutes your partner will call you back:

It is time to return now — but look once more around this world of your own calling ... then begin your journey back.

In the distance you can again see the doorway through which you entered into this world. As you reach the door, slowly open it again, and be aware that this realm of your dreams and visions is inside you, and that you can return here any time that you choose. Walk through this door now, and then close it again.

On the other side of the doorway you realize that you are not alone. You can feel the presence of another being. This might be a person, but it could also be a plant, an animal or a mythic being that is awaiting you here. It is an ally, a helper who knows your journey and your destination.

Look around for this helper, and greet him/her. Take some time to be with your helper. You can ask questions, and maybe he or she can help you to understand the images and experiences of your call ... (5 minutes)

It is time to say goodbye to your helper. Now that you know him/her you can always return here. Say goodbye.

Slowly let yourself return to the image of the well. The wind is blowing again through the branches of the old trees. When it touches the surface of the water, your images disappear. Let yourself stretch, and slowly return to the present.

When Parzival met the knights in the forest he was determined to follow his own call. He wanted to leave immediately for King Arthur's court to become a knight. When his mother realized that she could not keep him any longer, she gave him a miserable old horse and from sackcloth sewed him a Fool's hooded costume. She hoped that her son would be so mocked and beaten that he would return to her soon, but before Parzival left his mother she gave him some advice. He was to greet people, and avoid dark passageways. He should follow this advice on good behaviour, and try to win the love of women — and also, if possible, their ring.

When Parzival departed, the Queen's heart was broken. When she saw him ride off she lost consciousness and died. But Parzival did not know this, and, dressed as a Fool, he rode on into the world.

Chapter 6
The Fool

The Fool plays an important part in many myths and legends. He is an archetypal image of the soul. In a sense he embodies an inner attitude that can lead a person to an extraordinary destination on the journey of the hero.

We know the Fool as a circus clown who walks the arena with colourful clothes and shoes that are far too big. He makes fun of his more serious colleagues, and although he sometimes seems to be sad, there is a big smile painted on his white face. Through physical deformity or other extraordinary circumstances, the Fool is outside the normal course of events. He is a freak. General rules do not apply to him; he walks an extraordinary path. Seemingly naïve, he trusts only his own experience. Without inhibition, he steps beyond the limits of all order, and in so doing shows us our own limitations.

In the ceremonies and rituals of the American Indians the Fool, the 'Heyoehkah', plays an important role. He seems to do everything wrong. He walks backwards when everybody else walks forwards, and confronts people always with new opposites and contradictions. He is a craftsman of chaos who makes people unsure by showing the relativity and limitation of all order. At the same time, however, he opens the door to a new dimension of consciousness. It is his art, to go beyond the limits of order so that the new can come to be. That this is often a difficult task becomes clear through the account of Lame Deer, an American Indian Heyoehkah and Shaman:

> 'A clown in our language is called a heyoehkah. He is upside-down, backward-forward, a yes-and-no man, a

contrary-wise. Everybody can be made into a clown, from one day to another, whether he likes it or not. It is very simple to become a heyoehkah. All you have to do is dream about the lightning, the thunder-birds. You do this and when you wake up in the morning, you are a heyoehkah. There is nothing you can do about it.

If the thunder-beings want to put their power on the earth, among the people, they send a dream to a man, a vision about thunder and lightning. By this dream they appoint him to work his power for them in a human way. This is what makes him a heyoehkah. He doesn't even have to see the actual lightning or hear the thunder in his dream. If he dreams about a certain kind of horse coming towards him, about certain riders with grass in their hair or in their belts, he knows this comes from the wakinyan. Every dream which has some symbol of the thunder power in it will make you into a heyoehkah.

Suppose you have such a dream. What happens then? It is very unpleasant to talk about. What I mean is that a man who has dreamed about the thunder-birds, right away, the next morning, he's got a fear in him, a fear of performing his act. He has to act out his dream in public.

If I had a heyoehkah dream now which I had to re-enact, the thunder-being would put something in that dream that I'd be ashamed of. Ashamed to do in public, ashamed to own up to. Something that's going to make me not want to perform this act. And that is what's going to torment me. Having had that dream, getting up in the morning, at once I would hear this noise in the ground, just under my feet, that rumble of thunder, I'd know that before the day ends that thunder will come through and hit me, unless I perform the dream. I'm scared; I hide in the cellar; I cry; I ask for help, but there is no remedy until I have performed this act. Only this can free me. Maybe by doing this, I'll receive some power, but most people would just as soon forget about it.

The wise old people know that the clowns are thunder-dreamers, that the thunder-beings commanded them to act in a silly way, each heyoehkah according to his dream.'

(Peggy V. Beck & Anna L. Walters, *The Sacred)*

The Fool also plays an important role in the Tarot. Each card of the Tarot represents a basic human experience, and people lay out these cards to find answers to questions about their destiny. We know the images of the

Tarot from myths and fairy tales. There is, for instance, the Emperor and Empress, and Priest and the Hermit, the Sun, the Moon, the Lovers and also the Devil and Death. The succession of these cards corresponds with an esoteric path of initiation. Within this order, each card has its place which is marked by a Roman numeral — all, that is, except the Fool. He is outside this order. The symbol of his card is a circle, a symbol of wholeness which contains all possibilities. The circle can also be understood as the number Zero, and some authors place the Fool in front of the entire deck while others see him as number 22 at the end of the game.

It is in the nature of the Fool that he does not care about this order. Whenever we believe we understand him and give him a certain place within our order, he appears somewhere else, smiles and disappears again.

The Fool in the Tarot (from The Rider Tarot Deck, *US Games Systems Inc., New York, 1971).*

The Fool contains all experiences as a possibility. It is he who knows how to play the 'role of the Ego in 21 disguises to reveal the nature of being' (Lynda Saxon, *Craftsmen of Chaos*). As the Fool is ready to become all experiences and images, he can be seen as the master of the Tarot. Seemingly careless, he walks along an abyss. He may continue and fall, or he may turn around to walk uphill. His clothes are colourful; he is accompanied by a dog and in his hand he holds a flower.

A relative of the Fool is the youngest brother in fairy tales. He, too, is a dreamer. While his brothers follow their regular activities, he sits under a tree and dreams. And when there is an extraordinary task to be accomplished, to free a virgin from the teeth of a dragon or to get the water of life for the dying father, nobody thinks about him, the dreamer. But when his older brothers are unable to accomplish the task, the dreamer eventually sets out on the path. Like the Fool, he is not restricted by normal order. While his brothers have more important things to do than to listen to mysterious speaking animals and old women on the edge of the road, the dreamer follows these voices instinctively and therefore finds the right way to the water of life.

The Fool represents the possibility of going beyond the apparent boundaries of the ego to enter into an extraordinary realm. He is not limited by his knowledge or the fear of being embarrassed. He is always ready to learn and to realize the extraordinary. This attitude of the Fool is the wisdom of the beginner. In the words of the Zen Master Shunryu Suzuki Roshi, it is the 'beginner's mind'.

> 'If your mind is empty, it is always ready for anything; it is open for everything. In the beginner's mind there are many possibilities; in the expert's mind there are few ... In the beginner's mind there is no thought of "I have attained something". All self-centred thought limits our minds. When we have no thought of achievement, no thought of self, we are true beginners. Then we can really learn something.'
>
> (Shunryu Suzuki, *Zen Mind, Beginner's Mind*)

It is not easy to return to the beginner's mind. To be fully open to the moment and to trust one's own experience totally is to enter completely into the flow of life. As a personal attitude it enables us to go on an extraordinary journey.

Parzival, who rides in a Fool's costume into the world, is such a beginner. He is a Fool. As the son of a widow he is not caught up in the image of his father; he has to trust his own experiences.

At the beginning of the journey the Fool is often an imbecile. If he succeeds, however, in living through the diversity of his experiences, he can develop the wisdom of the Fool. In this way, he will become like the Shaman, a master of many worlds. Once he understands how to bring together the extraordinary with the ordinary, he becomes a 'Sacred Fool', a mediator between the worlds.

Chapter 7
Merlin

In many legends, Merlin is described as a 'Sacred Fool'. Through extraordinary circumstances, he also stands outside the normal order, but while Parzival is at the beginning of the journey, Merlin is already an old, wise man. He is a fool and a magician, and as a medicine man and priest he belongs to the tradition of the Celtic Bards and Druids.

For Emma Jung, Merlin represents the spiritual power of King Arthur's Round Table. Following Merlin's advice the old king, Uther Pendragon, established the Round Table. Around it, King Arthur gathered the best and bravest knights of his time. Merlin was a teacher and advisor to the Round Table (*see also* Jung and von Franz).

In Merlin's being, many worlds meet. He is light and dark at the same time. He knows the past and the future. While he is an old man he is also, as the king's advisor, a creation of nature: to his disciples he often appears as animal or plant, and he is closely connected with the world of fairies.

The challenges and adventures which the knights of the Round Table met often came from this other world of fairies and nature beings. It was a realm in which Merlin, as well as his lover Morgan le Fay, were at home. To follow their adventures in this realm, the knights had to leave the Round Table. Alone, they had to begin their journey and cross a threshold. As a Sacred Fool, Merlin knew these thresholds through his own experiences. For the knights who followed his call, he was a master of initiation.

Merlin was the child of a devil and a virgin. The remarkable conditions of his birth led him to a strange journey. In a medieval account, Robert de Boron tells Merlin's story:

Once the devils gathered in hell to decide how they could meet the spread of Christianity on earth. It was their task to spread darkness on earth. Through the work of the prophets and the hope of a second coming of Christ, they had lost a great deal of influence, and so they decided to send a prophet to earth to conceive a devil's sons.

In a human form a devil now came to the world, and found a young girl who seemed suitable for his purpose. This young woman was afraid of the devil's approaches and, when she suspected the intentions of the mysterious stranger, went to church to get advice from the priest. The priest knew at once that this could only be the devil, and so, knowing that the devil feared the light, he advised her to leave a candle burning in her room at night.

To confuse the girl, the devil brought great tragedies upon her family, and one night she forgot to light her candle. When she awoke the next day, she knew that something had happened; immediately, she went to church to confess. The priest said a prayer for her and sprinkled her with holy water. He drew the cross over her and to break the force of the devil he recommended a life of absolute purity. To be sure, however, the girl was thrown into prison. Here she gave birth to a son whom she called Merlin, after her father.

When the child was born it was covered with hair like an animal. Soon, however, it became clear that the child had unusual talents. In his being, the dark side of his father had united with the purity of his mother. From his father, Merlin knew everything that was; through his mother, he had the ability to tell the future. When his mother was brought to trial, the small Merlin suddenly began to speak, and succeeded in convincing the judges of the innocence and purity of his mother.

Because of his talents, Merlin was called later as an advisor to the court of the king. He told the king, Uther Pendragon, of the Round Table around which Jesus Christ had gathered his disciples. He told him of a second Round Table of Joseph of Arimathea, who had collected Christ's blood in a golden vessel. Following Merlin's advice, the king now established a third Round Table to gather a circle of chosen knights.

To celebrate the foundation of this Round Table, Uther Pendragon invited many knights and ladies. On this occasion, the king fell in love with the wife of the Duke of Tintagel, but as the young Duchess was already married she did not respond to Uther Pendragon's love. In his agony, the king turned to Merlin and asked for his help. Merlin played his dark side: through magic he transformed the king into a resemblance of the Duke, and in this guise Uther Pendragon succeeded in spending a night with the Duchess. In return for his help, Merlin claimed the child that would come from this union.

When the child was born it was called Arthur, and Merlin brought the boy to a knight who raised him together with his own son, Kay, near the woods. Sir Ector taught the boys the knightly virtues and the art of handling weapons. Arthur knew nothing of his origins.

In *The Once and Future King* T.H. White tells the story of how Arthur meets his teacher, Merlin. Once when the boys were playing in the forest, a tame falcon escaped. In order not to lose the bird, Arthur followed it into the woods and by the time night fell had completely lost his way. He curled up underneath a tree and fell asleep. When Arthur woke the next morning he heard a strange rattling. He followed the noise and in a clearing found a small house, totally overgrown with moss and ferns. In front of the house was a deep well, from which an old man was scooping water with a bucket.

'He was dressed in a flowing gown with fur tippets which had the signs of the zodiac embroidered over it with various cabalistic signs, such as triangles with eyes in them, queer crosse, leaves of trees, bones of birds and animals, and a planetarium whose stars shone like bits of looking-glass with the sun on them. He had a pointed hat like a dunce's cap, or like the headgear worn by ladies of that time, except that the ladies were accustomed to have a bit of veil floating from the top of it ... Merlyn had a long white beard and long white moustaches which hung down on either side of it. Close inspection showed that he was far from clean. It was not that he had dirty fingernails, or anything like that, but some large bird seemed to have been nesting in his hair ... This was the impression which he got from Merlyn. The old man was streaked with the droppings over his shoulders, among the stars and triangles of his gown, and a large spider was slowly lowering itself from the tip of his hat, as he gazed and slowly blinked at the little boy in front of him.'
(T.H. White, *The Once and Future King)*

The old man greeted the boy in a friendly way and it seemed as if he was expecting him. He took off his pointed hat and Arthur followed Merlin into his hut. Inside, there was great chaos. Between old leather-bound books hung a beehive, with bees flying in and out. In a corner Arthur saw live snakes, and moles and hedgehogs. On a large wardrobe were inkpots and many strange objects that Arthur had never seen before. On the drawers were signs like 'Mandragora', 'Mandrake', 'Old Man's Beard' and other names. When Merlin entered the room, a big owl flew to him and sat on his shoulder.

'Let's have some breakfast,' said Merlin and led the boy to a table where a hearty breakfast was ready. Arthur was very hungry and ate as much as he could. At the same time he was surprised. He asked Merlin why he had set the table for two. The old man watched him thoughtfully:

'Oh yes, how did I know to set breakfast for two? ... Now, ordinary people are born forwards in Time, if you understand what I mean, and nearly everything in the world goes forward too ... I, unfortunately, was born at the wrong end of Time, and I have to live backwards

> from in front, while surrounded by a lot of people living forwards from behind. Some people call it having second sight.'
>
> (T.H. White, *The Once and Future King*)

Arthur was fascinated by Merlin's art and from then on he often visited the old man. Merlin became his teacher.

While his stepfather, Sir Ector, taught Arthur the skills of a knight, Merlin opened the door to the hidden forces in nature. Like the Druids, who once educated the Celtic tribes, he taught the art of the fools and shamans. Through experiences, he showed him the oneness of all life. On a hot summer day, he transformed the boy in to a pike. He accompanied him as a large tench, and taught him to swim underwater and move with fins. In these movements, Arthur learned the power and suppleness of fish. On various occasions, Merlin transformed the boy into a hunting bird, an ant, a wild goose, a mole, and many other animals. In each shape Arthur experienced the power and quality of the animal within himself. Like a fool, he learned to go beyond his own limitations and enter totally into experience.

Several years later the old king, Uther Pendragon, died and throughout the country a search was begun to find a new king. In order to find the best knight, a tournament was arranged to which Sir Ector was also invited. The contest lasted many days, but no clear winner could be found. Then, on Christmas Day, a huge rock in which a sword was lodged appeared in front of the door of the cathedral. Whoever could pull the sword from the rock would become the new king.

Knights and noblemen from all over the country tried to pull the sword from the rock, but hard as they tried the sword did not move. It was as if the steel was fused with the rock. When, on the following day, a new tournament was about to begin, Sir Ector realized that he had left his sword at an inn the night before. He asked Arthur to ride off and get it, but when Arthur reached the inn he found all doors and windows locked. As hard as he tried, he could not enter the house.

On his way back, Arthur rode across the cathedral yard and saw the rock with the sword in it. He did not want to return empty-handed, and as he could not find his stepfather's sword he wanted to try to pull this sword from the rock. Arthur got off his horse, and with strong hands grabbed the handle of the sword. He pulled as hard as he could but the sword did not move. With sweat running down his face, the boy pulled again with all his might. 'Oh Merlin,' he called in desperation, 'help me to pull this sword from the rock!' But the sword did not move. Suddenly he heard a strange rushing noise:

> All round the churchyard there were hundreds of old friends. They rose over the church wall all together, like the Punch and Judy ghosts of remembered days, and there were badgers and nightingales and vulgar crows and hares and wild geese and falcons and fishes and dogs and dainty unicorns and solitary wasps and corkindrills and hedgehogs and griffins and the thousand other animals he had met. They loomed round the church wall, the lovers and helpers of the Wart [Arthur], and they all spoke solemnly in turn. Some of them had come from the banners in the church, where they were painted in heraldry, some from the waters and the sky and the fields about — but all, down to the smallest shrew mouse, had come to help on account of love. Wart felt his power grow.
>
> 'Put your back into it,' said a Luce [pike] off one of the heraldic banners, 'as you once did when I was going to snap you up. Remember that power springs from the nape of the neck.'
>
> 'What about those forearms,' asked a badger gravely, 'that are held together by a chest? Come along, my dear embryo, and find your tool.'
>
> A Merlin sitting on top of the yew tree cried out, 'Now then, Captain Wart, what is the first law of the foot? I thought I once heard something about never letting go?'
>
> 'Don't work like a stalling woodpecker,' urged a Tawny Owl affectionately. 'Keep up a steady effort, my duck, and you will have it yet.'
>
> A white-front said, 'Now, Wart, if you were once able to fly the great North Sea, surely you can co-ordinate a few little wing-muscles here and there? Fold your powers together, with the spirit of your mind, and it will come

> out like butter. Come along, homo sapiens, for all we humble friends of yours are waiting here to cheer.'
>
> (T.H. White, *The Once and Future King)*

Arthur felt the strength of his allies. He took the sword in his hands and heaved it out of the rock. During his time with Merlin he had learned to become one with the power of the animals; he had experienced the power of these beings within himself.

Arthur now became the king of the knights and the leader of the Round Table, from where the knights went out to find their adventures in mysterious realms. Merlin, however, said farewell to the knights and withdrew into nature. The knights must not think that he had arranged their mysterious encounters. He wanted them to believe their own experience. In the solitude of the forest, he now explored the course of the stars and he sang of future events. To his disciples, however, Merlin's wisdom remained alive in plants and animals. He had met them in many forms before. Now they listened to him in the sound of the wind in the leaves of the oaks, in the sounds of animals, and the mysterious gushing of springs from the earth. His being could still be experienced in nature.

In their adventures the knights of the Round Table continued to meet creatures and beings from Merlin's nature kingdom. Often these beings also came from the fairy realm of his lover, Morgan le Fay.

Merlin's wisdom was never communicated as cognitive knowledge. It was a knowledge of experience, a deep communion with the forces of a hidden world. Merlin taught the art of transformation; he led his disciples beyond the boundaries of the 'small self' and taught them the oneness of all life. His wisdom is still alive today. The power of many Shamans and Medicine Men and Women is also based on this ability to become one with the force of another being. This may be animal or plant, it may be fire, or the spirit of a god or ancestor. As the Shaman becomes one with the spirit of another being, its powers come alive in him. Like this he can perform seemingly impossible tasks.

In the Celtic 'Song of Amergin' which is ascribed to a disciple of Merlin, Merlin's art comes alive:

I am a stag: of seven tines,
I am a flood: across a plain,
I am a wind: on a deep lake,
I am a tear: the sun lets fall,
I am a hawk; above the cliff,
I am a thorn: beneath the nail,
I am a wonder: among flowers,
I am a wizard: who but I
Sets the cool head aflame with smoke?

I am a spear: that roars of blood,
I am a salmon: in a pool,
I am a lure from paradise,
I am a hill: where poets walk,
I am a boar: ruthless and red,
I am a breaker: threatening doom,
I am a tide: that drags to death,
I am an infant: who but I
Peeps from the unhewn dolmen arch?

I am the womb: of every holt,
I am the blaze: on every hill,
I am the queen: of every hive,
I am the shield: for every head,
I am the tomb: of every hope.

The images of the Celtic 'Song of Amergin' can be a doorway to our own experience. If we allow ourselves to experience these images, we can discover Merlin's art of transformation within ourselves.

It is best to begin this exploration with deep relaxation, during which you reach all parts of your body with awareness. While a partner reads (or a cassette plays) the 'Song of Amergin' again, you can awaken these images in your imagination.

Imagine your body changing with each image. To awaken the power of these images in your body you can also find postures that correspond with each picture. Like a shaman you can thus become one with the power of the bird, the wind or the fire, and enter into a creative process with your own body.

Chapter 8
The Path

Parzival was in good spirits as he rode into the world. In his being he had the capacity to become a Sacred Fool, who is called to go beyond the limits of his time to realize the extraordinary. But initially, Parzival was just imbecile. His mother had sewn him a fool's costume so he would return to her, mocked by the world. But the fool's costume, designed to hinder him in a world of knights, led him straight towards his true destination. With the unabashed openness of a fool, he was able to ride straight into the centre of knighthood to meet the King of the Knights.

Initially, Parzival followed his mother's advice. As she had warned him of dark passageways he rode for a whole day along a river which Wolfram described as being so shallow that a chicken could have easily waded through it. When he crossed the river the next day, he came to a large tent. Parzival believed that this was a church.

The tent was furnished with precious carpets, and when the boy opened the curtain he found the Duchess of Lalant, only half-dressed, resting on a bed. Parzival was delighted by her beauty, and when he saw a ring on her finger he remembered his mother's advice: he kissed the sleeping Duchess, and with force took the ring off her hand and a brooch from her dress. When the Duchess awoke, Parzival told her of his mother. He was hungry and asked her for something to eat. The Duchess was horrified and amazed as she watched how the beautiful boy in his fool's costume devoured two partridge stews and her husband's wine. Jeschute knew that her husband, Duke Orilus, would kill the boy if he found him in her tent. She begged him to return the ring and leave, but Parzival finished his meal in his own time, mounted his horse and rode away.

When the Duke returned and saw the empty bowls, he believed that his wife had entertained a lover. The Duchess told him of the beautiful boy with his rough shirt and calf-leather boots, and in tears she claimed her innocence. But when Orilus saw her ring gone, he became furious. He tore up her precious clothes and broke her decorated saddle. Until he was avenged, she was to follow him like a beggar on an old nag.

Parzival knew nothing of this. Unconcerned, he continued on his way. He greeted all people he met, and always added that his mother had advised him so to do.

Once when Parzival rode through a forest, he heard the sound of desperate cries. As he came closer, he found a young woman with a dead knight on her knees. In agony, she tore the hair from her head, and in tears she told him of her lover who had lost his life in battle with Duke Orilus. To prove his love, she had sent him into battle. Parzival could not comprehend that the knight was dead and that he was not moving at all. He shuddered in the face of death and, as he was sorry for the woman, he wanted to avenge the death immediately. But to protect the boy from the dangerous battle with the Duke, she sent him in the wrong direction. When he departed she asked him for his name, but Parzival did not know it. His mother had called him 'cher fils' and 'bon fils', and when the young woman heard this she recognized him as her cousin. 'Your name is Parzival,' she said, 'and it means "Pierce through the heart".' She told him now of Gahmuret and Herzeloyde, and the wound that went right through his mother's heart when he left. She told him that he was destined to ride right through the middle of all powers of this world. Then she showed him the way to Nantes.

When evening came, Parzival reached the hut of a

fisherman. In exchange for his accommodation, he gave the fisherman the brooch he had taken from Duchess Jeschute, and early in the morning he continued his journey. He rode all day, but the road to Nantes never seemed to end. His horse was tired and he began to suffer under the mockery of the people. Finally, in the evening, he saw the endless blue of the sea and the golden towers of Nantes. This was the place where King Arthur held court with the bravest knights. Soon he would be a knight too, and once again he spurred his horse to gallop.

At the threshold to the world of knights, Parzival encountered the Red Knight. As he reached the town wall a gate opened and a radiant Red Knight came riding from the town. His armour was gleaming red in the evening sun, and red was the color of this mighty horse. His saddle was of red velvet and gold. His iron shield, as well as his lance and sword, was flaming red. Parzival was delighted. Fascinated, he stared at this wild rider who held a golden chalice in his hand. But the Red Knight, too, was surprised at the strange appearance of the boy in his fool's costume.

Sir Ither of Gaheviez was a nephew of King Arthur. To reinforce his claim to an inheritance in Brittany, he had taken a golden chalice from the king's table. On his horse he had ridden up right to the king's table, and in his insolence had spilt wine over the queen's dress. The Red Knight asked Parzival to bring a message to the king. He was to tell King Arthur that the Red Knight regretted spilling wine over the queen's dress, and that if a knight of the Round Table wished to avenge the dishonor and regain the king's cup, he would meet him in battle in front of the town gate.

Parzival was pleased by this demand, but when he entered the king's palace he found the knights in great disarray. Enthusiastically, he observed the precious clothes of the knights and ladies and the many chandeliers in the hall. He had never seen so much beauty and so much wealth. 'I see many Arthurs here,' he said, 'but who will make me a knight now?'

Iwanet, the queen's nephew, led him to King Arthur, who sat at the end of the table lost in thought. By now the beauty of the boy with his strange appearance and his hunting spear had caught the knights' attention. The king, too, was touched by Parzival's innocence and beauty. When Parzival had passed on the message of the Red Knight, he asked the king to make him a knight. When he asked, however, for the armour and the horse of the Red Knight, the king smiled in surprise. He was not authorized to give away the belongings of his knights. The court's seneschal, who wanted to get rid of the strange boy, encouraged Parzival to go and get the armour himself. If he succeeded, the king would grant him the right to wear the red armour.

As if in a dream, Parzival bowed to the king. Immediately he wanted to return to the town's gate where the Red Knight was waiting for him, but as Parzival crossed the courtyard of the palace he heard the laugh of a young woman, who waved to him. Lady Cunneware was the sister of Duke Orilus. Years ago she had promised never to laugh again until she found the man who was destined to achieve the highest possible feat, and when she saw the beautiful boy in his fool's costume and his calf-leather boots, she began to laugh from her heart. But the rude seneschal did not understand, and was so furious that this fool had caused her to laugh that he hit her in the face with a stick. Parzival was ready to throw his spear at the seneschal, but rode instead to the gate of the town where the Red Knight was awaiting him. 'I have given your message to the king,' he said, 'Now give me your horse and your armour because I too wish to become a knight. King Arthur wants you to know that he has given his consent from now on for me to wear your armour.'

The Red Knight laughed at the foolish boy, but when Parzival reached for the reins of his red horse he hit the boy with the shaft of his lance, and Parzival went tumbling through the flowers. Parzival was furious. His blood boiled. Dreamlike he reached for his hunting spear and threw it with such force that the knight tumbled and fell lifeless from his horse. Parzival's spear had stabbed him through the visor of his helmet. It had penetrated through his eye socket and down to his neck. Parzival could not comprehend what had happened — he could not understand why the knight no longer moved, and he felt anxious.

With the help of a young page, he took the armour from the dead knight and put it on, but he refused to take off the fool's costume that his mother had made for him. Iwanet gave him the sword and lance of the Red Knight and showed him how to use the weapons. When Parzival mounted the horse in his red armour he believed himself at the height of his dreams. He gave Iwanet King Arthur's golden cup and asked him to offer his services to Lady Cunneware, who had recognised his true nature. Then he rode off.

From his outer appearance Parzival was now a knight, but inwardly he was still a boy (and under the armour, of course, he still wore the fool's costume). The people who before had mocked him, now greeted him with respect. Parzival galloped all day because he did not know how to control the powerful horse. Totally exhausted, he reached that night the castle of Sir Gurnemanz of Graharz. His horse seemed to know his way there and when Parzival rode into the courtyard he found the white-haired Gurnemanz under a linden tree. The old man greeted him kindly, and invited him to stay. He threw a sparrow hawk into the air, and soon knights appeared to lead the guest into the main house.

At first Parzival refused to descend from his horse. 'A king has made me a knight,' he said, 'and I will not descend from this horse no matter what happens. But I will greet you, as my mother has taught me to do.' Finally Parzival did descend from his horse, and when he took off his shining armour his gaudy fool's costume appeared. Everyone was greatly surprised, but old Gurnemanz took the boy into his house and called for a festive dinner to be prepared. Parzival was very hungry and while helping himself heartily, he told his host about his mother, the encounter with Duchess Jeschute and his battle with the Red Knight at King Arthur's court.

Sir Gurnemanz was a teacher of knights, and by the following day he had already begun to teach the boy the knightly skill and virtues. He taught him how to use his sword and the skills of combat. Parzival showed great talent, and in the tournaments he was soon superior to all the other boys and knights. Sir Gurnemanz also taught him etiquette; he advised him to keep his mother's image in his heart but not to talk about her all the time. He taught him how to participate in the Mass, and to unite courage with mercy. He advised him always to be moderate and warned him not to ask unnecessary questions; and finally, gurnemanz explained to him that man and woman are a unity, and asked him to take women into his heart and honor them. In following his teacher's advice, Parzival took off his gaudy fool's costume — and with it a part of his innocence as well. He now exchanged the nature of the Fool for the role of a Knight.

C.G. Jung has called this part of a person, which is directed towards the world, the 'Persona'. Originally, this Latin term described the mask which an actor wore in theatre to impersonate a specific character. In Jung's *Analytical Psychology*, the term 'Persona' describes the role which a person plays on the stage of life and through which he engages the world. At the beginning of life, this persona is largely defined by the expectations of his environment. The child learns to adapt in order to relate to others. It begins to play one role (or more). In the course of development, a person thus learns to distinguish these roles from the essence of his own being. Apart from the role he plays in contact with other people, he becomes aware of his own essence. Through this, his judgement will no longer be exclusively defined by the expectations of his environment. He develops his own individuality.

The persona is often defined through a social role. A specific 'mask' corresponds with the profession of a doctor, a psychotherapist, a student or a craftsman. If a person is totally identified with this mask, however — if he forgets that he is a person who is able to play a particular role — he cannot develop his own identity. He is then caught up in an 'image' and is estranged from himself.

Parzival, too, is now totally identified with the role of the knight. The loss of his colorful clothes reflects the loss of access to the original qualities of his being. His one-sided identification with the role of knight will become his destiny. In the course of the story he will, however, succeed in going beyond the limitations of this role and developing his own individuality.

Old Gurnemanz did not like to see him depart again. He would have liked Parzival to marry his daughter, and his departure was like losing a son. Liaze was a beautiful girl and Parzival grew to like her, but inwardly he felt a stirring restlessness: the width of the valley seemed too narrow, its breadth too short, the green of the meadows and trees too pale, and the red of his armour too colorless. He yearned to move out into the world. He longed to find again his mother whom he lad left unconscious on the bridge of Soltane — he did not know of her death. After several weeks, he took leave of Gurnemanz and his daughter and, as a knight, he went out into the world.

Chapter 9
Condwiramurs

Parzival left his horse's reins loose as it carried him through rocky mountains. Again and again, the image of the beautiful Liaze appeared in his mind's eye and his thoughts began to wander. Old Gurnemanz had taught him that man and woman are a unity, that they cannot be separated from one another. His knightly education was, in essence, education of his manhood. In relation to Liaze, however, his feminine side had been touched — Liaze had left a deep impression on him.

Parzival's horse followed the course of a torrential river, and in the evening he reached the town of Pelrapeire at the river's mouth. Here he found the feminine in the form of a young princess in distress. Her country was devastated by enemies and the town was under siege by a king who wanted to force the queen, Condwiramurs, to marry him. Over a narrow suspension bridge Parzival crossed the river, and arrived at the gates of the town. Even though he knocked loudly, he had to wait a long time. When the heavy door was finally opened, he found a crowd of armed warriors, their faces ash-grey and their bodies affected by hunger. For weeks no food had entered the town, and distress and sickness threatened the people who remained loyal to their queen.

The houses and streets had fallen into ruin. Parzival saw a cathedral peopled by helpless monks and anxious nuns. In front of the palace was an old linden tree, and in its shade he was freed of his armour. The queen greeted her guest and led him to the palace. Parzival was deeply touched by her beauty and the grief reflected in her features. For a long time they sat silently together. Gurnemanz (who was her uncle) had taught Parzival not to ask unnecessary questions, and only after a long time did the queen begin to speak.

When Parzival awoke in the night his room was lit by candles. In a silken garment Condwiramurs was kneeling beside his bed. But in Wolfram's words, she had not come to him for the love which turns virgins into women, but to ask him for help in her despair. Tearfully, she told him how she had lost castles and counties to King Clamide, who now besieged her town. Parzival promised to fight Clamide. He asked her not to kneel in front of him and invited her to lie beside him. He promised not to act dishonorably, and, without touching each other, they lay side by side on his bed.

The next morning Parzival left the town to fight with Kingrun, the seneschal of King Clamide. Kingrun was a much-feared knight, and they fought so violently that their saddle laces tore and their shields split into pieces. The knights continued their battle with swords. In the end, however, Kingrun had to surrender to the Red Knight. Parzival spared his life and sent him to King Arthur's court. There he was to offer his services to the young lady, Cunneware.

When Parzival returned to the town, Condwiramurs asked him to marry her. 'I will never be the wife of another knight,' she said to the assembled people, 'except the one that I hold in my arms.' In the port of Pelrapeire, they now saw the sails of a large merchant ship bringing vital food to the starving town. Inside as well as outside, the spell was broken. As the new ruler, Parzival gave food to the people, even the prisoners were generously supplied with food and drink.

In the meantime, King Clamide had moved with a large army to the outskirts of the town to await their surrender. When the prisoners were set free, however, they praised the new king's generosity and with their drunken stammering and red faces, told King Clamide of the delicacies and wine they had enjoyed in the town. Clamide angrily challenged Parzival, but he, too, had to surrender and was sent to King Arthur's court to offer his services to Cunneware.

The following night Parzival shared his bed again with the Queen. For three nights, however, they did not touch each other. Their relationship was a spiritual one and only after three nights did he remember that his mother had advised him to take a woman into his arms. So now they twined their arms and legs and discovered the eternal play of yin and yang which keeps our world in balance.

Parzival's relationship with Condwiramurs was of a kind that was absolutely new in the Middle Ages. It was based neither on a church marriage nor on the passion of the senses. It was a love which went far beyond the ideals of its time. We can understand this relationship in connection with the movement of the Cathars and the Troubadours of Provence in whose prayers and songs a new, occidental spirituality began to emerge. The Troubadours were the Minne singers at the Courts of Provence who, as the voice of the 'Gaia Scienca' — the happy sciences — celebrated a new image of man. Instead of asceticism and detachment from the world, they affirmed the whole of human nature. As followers of a mystical eroticism, they praised love as a realization of the divine. Under their influence, the Minne became a virtue and a new ideal came to be. Alongside the previous overemphasis of the male in knighthood, the feminine now began to emerge, a development also advancing within the church, where veneration of the Mother Mary was growing.

The 'Fideli d'Amore' — the believers of love — gathered as followers of a Christian esoteric of love at the Minne Courts of Provence. Like the knights of the Grail, they wore white and red clothes. In the symbolic language of alchemy, white was the color of the sun and red the color of the moon. In their songs, they praised the relationship of sun and moon, of masculine and feminine, as a revelation of the divine. In their mysteries, they sought to awaken equally the male and the female forces within a person. At the time of the Crusades, many of these movements were suppressed by the church. Its members were often tortured and cruelly murdered. Instead of giving in to the force of the church, however, the last Cathars jumped into the flames of the stake, crying out 'God is Love!'.

In Wolfram's epic poem, Condwiramur's colors are also white and red. 'She was like a rose covered in dew whose beauty was shining with splendor. White and red at the same time ...'. Her name — *conduire amour* — means 'guide to love'. In her communion with Parzival, she awakens the feminine side of his being

In each person, there are feminine and masculine forces. In Chinese philosophy these forces are called Yin and Yang, and through their interplay the flow of life — the Tao — unfolds. C.G. Jung called these forces within a person Anima and Animus. 'Anima' means soul: to a man she is his inner feminine image of the soul, which unconsciously influences his attitudes and beliefs. 'Animus' originally means spirit, wind or breath: it is the masculine, spiritual and intellectual force in a woman's soul. As these forces are at odds with a consciously-lived gender role, they are largely unconscious. If, however, a person succeeds in experiencing and inwardly uniting these contradictory forces, he may reveal himself as a guide to the deeper levels of the soul. In this way, the interplay of Yin and Yang can unfold as a creative process.

You can discover the qualities of these inner forces on a Guided Journey. During this journey I will suggest some images to you. Let these images come into focus in your mind's eye as sharply as they can. If you have difficulty in visualizing, let yourself imagine these images in whatever way is best for you.

To begin, find a comfortable position, close your eyes, and relax. Let your breath flow easily.

As you continue to relax, imagine the image of a burning candle, shining brightly in the darkness. Let yourself feel the atmosphere of a candle in a dark room.

Let go of this image now and imagine the color red in front of your right eye, and in front of your left eye the color white. Red in front of your right eye, and white in front of your left eye. Now imagine the color white in front of your right eye, and the color red in front of your left eye.

Then, let go of these colors. Take a deep breath and imagine a golden chalice filled with red wine. A gold chalice filled with red wine.

Let go of this image now, and imagine a sword — a sword such as the knights of King Arthur's Round Table might have carried.

Then, let this image disappear. Take another deep breath and begin to see the image of a ripe apple. Let yourself explore this crisp ripe apple. Look at its colors and its shape, and even smell it if you can.

Imagine that you are taking a crunchy bite of this apple. Discover its taste and its consistency. Then let go of this image again.

Take another deep breath and let the image of the moon appear in front of your mind's eye. Imagine the moon and the light and the atmosphere which surrounds the moon.

And then imagine the sun, as it rises on a crystal clear morning above the horizon. Let yourself see the light of the sun as it rises in the early morning.

Then, let go of these images. Take a deep breath and imagine the movement of walking in your own body. Let yourself feel this movement in the play of your muscles.

Imagine that you are walking along a path that leads you to the sea. It is hot. You can feel the earth under your feet and you can smell the scent of fresh herbs and grasses.

Focus your awareness on this movement of walking.

In the movements of your muscles you can feel your own gender. As a man you can feel in this movement your own masculinity; as a woman you can feel your own femininity in your body.

Your path leads you down to the beach. In the distance you can see a small beach café. There are palm trees here, and you lie down to rest in the shade of a palm tree. You can feel the soft and warm sand under your body, and the wind that plays in the leaves of the tree. Waves are rolling onto the white sand, and it is so peaceful here that you begin to drift ... and dream ...

As you awake you take a deep breath. You do not know how long you have been sleeping here. You stretch a little, and then you make a strange discovery: As you begin to move your body you realize that while you were sleeping your body has changed its gender. If you were a man before, you find yourself now in the body of a woman. If you were a woman before, you are now in the body of a man. Slowly you begin to feel this change in your body: in your arms and legs, in your shoulders and your chest; in your hips and thighs and in your face. As you begin to move you can feel the changes in your body.

You now have ten minutes to explore all the possibilities and experiences with this new body. In your fantasy this is a long time, and there are no limits to our imagination. All possible and impossible clothes are at your disposal. And your journey of exploration begins now ...

... Wherever you are, you find a large mirror now.

Slowly you approach this mirror and you look at yourself in your new body ...

You take another step forward, and as you lift your hand to touch your reflection, you realize that the mirror is penetrable, like the surface of still water that reflects your own image.

With your hand you slowly move through the surface of this mirror, then with your arms and shoulders, realizing that your body is changing shape again ... slowly you walk through the mirror, and as you reach the other side you notice that your body has changed to its original shape again.

You take a few deep breaths, stretch, and when you are ready, you open your eyes again.

As we awaken both the masculine and the feminine, we step beyond the polarity of yin and yang. We begin to live the Tao. For a man the feminine — and for a woman the masculine — is a mediator to the contents of the unconscious. They are a complimentary forces that can lead us to wholeness and a deeper level of our being.

For Parzival, the encounter with Condwiramurs was an access to a deeper realm. Only for a short time was he the king in Pelrapeire. Although the country was blossoming under his rule, he began to long again for his mother whom he had left behind in Soltane. Eventually he left Condwiramurs, but he promised to return as soon as he had found his mother.

On Parzival's journey, however, there seemed to be no return. He would never return to Pelrapeire and he would never find his mother again. Searching for his mother, Parzival came to the Grail Castle which can only be entered unknowingly and unintentionally.

Chapter 10
The Sacred Wound

As Parzival enters the world of the Grail, the atmosphere of the story changes. It becomes mystic and magic. It seems as if he stepped into the realm of a dream. How far away this realm was from Parzival's normal consciousness is demonstrated by the long distance he rode without holding the reins of his horse. 'It is farther than a bird could have flown in a day.'

In Richard Wagner's version, Parzival says, as he enters into the world of the Grail: 'I'm hardly walking and seem to have gone so far,' and his companion answers, 'You see, son, time has become space here.'

Parzival enters into a realm of images and dreams that lies far beyond the limits of linear thinking. It is an inner space of the soul, a state of consciousness where time and space, the co-ordinates of waking consciousness, become one. The past continues to exist and the future can already be felt approaching. The realm of the Grail is not a geographical place, but a state of consciousness, a realm beyond our waking consciousness. This 'realm beyond' played an important role in the mythology of the Celts. It was a land beneath the earth where the gods dwelt, or a land beyond the water or under the waves.

Much has been written about this 'other world' and the wealth of symbols in the Grail Castle. There are literary and cultural historical studies, but also psychological, esoteric and Christian interpretations as well as astrological and alchemical ones. If we understand the realm of the Grail as an inner space, however, all interpretations become less important. The analysis of an inner condition can never correspond with the experience of an inner space. If we try to understand this other world by linear thinking, we will miss its essence. Far more important that the explanation and the understanding of these images and symbols is the question of what these can evoke inside us. You cannot eat the description of an apple, and inner spaces can only be experienced.

During the time I wrote about Parzival's visit to the Grail Castle, I experienced a great deal. The deeper I entered into the images of the Grail Mystery, the less important all explanations and interpretations became. Like Parzival, I did not understand the meaning of these images for long periods of time. Through dreams, in dance, and by inner journeys of discovery, however, I made some very personal discoveries. The images in my mind's eye began to have an effect on me.

The mystery of the Grail mirrors an ancient ritual which recalls the Christian last Supper, or the Mysteries of Eleusis. The Cathars and Troubadours knew about these mysteries. When their communities were threatened by the Crusades, they hoped to preserve these mysteries in the form of legends (see Rudolf Meyer, *Zum Raum Wird Hier Die Zeit*).

To experience the effect of the mystery of the Grail, we need to enter into this 'other realm' of images and dreams. Like Parzival, we can only enter this realm unknowingly.

When Parzival left Pelrapeire, he rode for a whole day. In the evening he came to a desert landscape where neither trees nor bushes nor grass grew. The earth was burnt and dried up. At the foot of a mountain, Parzival came to a river. He hoped to find a path here that would lead him to his mother, but as there was no bridge he rode along the river. In the middle of the water he saw a boat, anchored, with two men on board. They were casting their nets into the depths of the river, and in an apparently negligent manner were letting the boat drift. The men were dressed in precious clothes. While one of them held the nets in his hands, the other sat motionless at the far end of the boat. He was supported by many cushions and on his large hat he sported a peacock's feather. Both men's faces, however, seemed sad and careworn.

When Parzival came closer, the men became restless and carelessly let the fish escape from their nets. Parzival asked them for a place to spend the night, and the rich fisherman answered that there was only one place within thirty miles. 'I know of no habitation beside the lake or inland for thirty miles. Nearby stands a lone mansion. I urge you to go there ... If you find the right way there I shall take care of you myself this evening.'

Parzival continued alongside the mountain and soon he saw the many towers of a castle. The bridge across the moat was up, but when he called out that the fisherman had sent him here the bridge was lowered, and through a large gate he rode into the castle.

Inside, Parzival found tall grass and was surprised to find no traces of knightly games and tournaments. The knights of the castle gathered around their guest and unburdened him of his heavy armour. A servant brought Parzival a coat of red silk from Queen Repanse of Schoye, and it was almost as if they had expected him. The people in the castle seemed to be sad, however, and when Parzival had washed the rust from his armour off his face, he was like a ray of light in their midst.

Parzival was now led into the palace which was blazing with light from a hundred many-candled chandeliers. On each of a hundred cushions sat four people. In front of each was a priceless carpet from the East. There were three marble fireplaces in which Aloe wood was burning, and the sound of many voices filled the hall. When Parzival entered the hall all voices became silent. On a preciously-ornamented bed in the middle of the hall he recognized the fisherman who had directed him to the castle. He was still supported by a pile of cushions and seemed to be in great pain. His life was one of great suffering, and in spite of the open fires he seemed to be cold. His coat was made of precious sable fur and his black sable hat was decorated with gold and red rubies. The Fisher King sat up in his bed and asked his guest to sit with him.

Suddenly a door opened. A squire in battered armour entered the hall carrying a lance. He bowed in all directions and carried the lance slowly through the hall. It seemed to remind the knights of a great disaster, and the hall was filled now with cries and wailing. As the knight approached, Parzival saw a drop of blood appearing from the tip of the lance and dripping down along its shaft. When the squire left the room again the wailing stopped, and Parzival was left surprised by the things he had seen.

Then another door opened and two women in reddish-brown dresses entered the hall. They wore wreaths of flowers in their hair, and in their hands they held a candle. Two more women in red-brown dresses brought two ivory stools which they placed in front of the king and his guest. Then more women entered dressed in green gowns which were gathered by richly-ornamented girdles. They brought a precious tabletop carved from jacinth — tawny and translucent — which they placed on top of the ivory stools. Then another six women entered. On a cloth they carried two sharp knives which were placed on the table in front of the King and Parzival.

Finally the Queen entered the hall. Her dress was made of Arabian silk and her beauty was shining like the dawn. On a green cloth of silk she carried the embodiment of perfection, the beginning and end of all human endeavor — the Holy Grail. The light of the Grail radiated throughout the hall and it seemed as if the light of the candles paled — just as the light of the stars becomes pale when the moon is rising.

The Queen walked slowly through the hall and then placed the Grail in front of the Fisher King. There were two circles now, each of twelve women, and Parzival was amazed by the radiant beauty of the Queen. 'It was she who sent me the coat,' he thought to himself.

The Grail as a chalice is a symbol of wholeness. Shown here is the eighteenth-century Ardagh Chalice from Ireland (from John Matthews: The Grail. The Search for Eternity, *London, Thames & Hudson, 1981).*

A hundred tables with white tablecloths were now placed in front of the knights. Four chariots brought golden vessels to everyone, and the King and Parzival washed their hands in bowls. Parzival saw now that in front of the Grail a rich feast was ready. Whatever people desired was there. There were warm dishes and cold ones, known and unknown food with selected spices from all over the world. Whatever people desired, whether it was mulberry wine or wine from grapes or other delicacies — through the power of the Grail their cups were filled miraculously, and a hundred servants distributed the food among the ladies and the knights. Parzival was deeply surprised by the events he witnessed. As his teacher had taught him not to ask unnecessary questions, however, and as he was tired he remained silent.

When the feast was over, the king handed Parzival a sword whose handle was carved from a single ruby. The king himself had carried this sword in many battles before he was wounded. Parzival thanked the king, and when he held the sword in his hands it seemed as if all eyes were resting on him. But again Parzival did not want to ask any questions. He did not ask the king about his suffering or about the miracles he had witnessed in the Grail Castle.

The queen and her women bowed to the king, and in silence they carried the Grail from the room. When they opened the door, Parzival saw a venerable old man on a bed. His appearance was beautiful, his hair white like the mist. It was to him that the queen carried the Grail.

When the king said goodbye to his guest, Parzival was led into a beautiful room and undressed by pages. Women brought mulberry wine and fruits, and soon he fell into a restless sleep. All night he was tormented by fearsome dreams, and when he awoke it was already late in the morning. There was silence everywhere, and to his calls he received no answer.

Parzival found that the precious clothes he had received the day before had gone. His sword and armour were lying in front of his bed, also the sword of the Grail King. Again Parzival called out for the people of the castle, but no-one answered. Alone, he put on his heavy armour, and when he tried to return to the main hall he found the doors locked. Only the door to the outside was open. Outside Parzival found his horse saddled and his shield and lance leaning against a wall. The grass in the courtyard was flattened now, and it seemed as if many knights had gathered here to leave the castle. Parzival called out again, but still he received no answer.

In anger he mounted his horse. The castle gate was open and he rode out of it at a gallop. Parzival had almost crossed the moat when suddenly the castle gate closed with a big crash, and the drawbridge was pulled up with such force that he almost fell with his horse into the abyss. With a huge jump Parzival reached the other side. Furiously he called out for the guardian of the gate. He wanted to know the secrets of this castle. From the castle wall he heard the voice of a knight: 'Ride on, you goose, and bear the hatred of the sun. If only you had opened your mouth to ask the king about his suffering. Now you have lost your honor and your praise!' To his questions Parzival received no more answers. The gate of the castle remained closed. Confused, Parzival followed the tracks of the horses. He wanted to catch up with the knights but eventually lost their tracks on the dry ground.

After some time he heard the sound of a woman's cries, and found a woman who held a dead, embalmed knight in her arms. It was Sigune. Her head was shaven and her cries echoed through the barren land. Surprised and in despair, she looked at the stranger and asked him where he had come from. Parzival told her about the castle where he had spent the night, but Sigune did not believe him:

> 'There is no house or dwelling for thirty miles — except a single castle. It is the most beautiful on earth! Only a person who is destined to do so can enter this castle, and no-one in search of it will ever find it. The old Titurel had this castle built and he passed it on to his son Frimutel, who died in service for the love of a lady. His children are now in great despair. One of them has chosen the life of a hermit. His brother, Anfortas, is the king of Munsalvasche. He is wounded and can neither walk nor ride, he can neither rest nor stand.'

Parzival told Sigune of the miraculous events in the Grail Castle. And then Sigune recognized him, and when she saw his sword she was overjoyed. She believed that he had redeemed the Grail King through a heartfelt question. But Parzival said: 'I did not ask!'.

Disappointed and angry, she looked at him in his red armour: 'Shame on you,' she said, 'that you did not show mercy and ask your host about his suffering!' You saw the king's suffering, saw the bleeding lance, and still you did not ask! You are cursed now, and although you are still alive your happiness is gone.'

Sigune told him about the meaning of his sword: for the first blow it will hold, but at the second blow it will break. Only Trebouchet, the blacksmith of Karnant who made this sword, could put it together again. And before Parzival left, Sigune told him too of the death of his mother and how she died when he had left her. In despair and without direction, Parzival rode on.

As in a dream, Parzival had witnessed the images of the Grail Mystery. He had seen the suffering of the king and the bleeding lance. He had experienced the life-giving force of the Grail with his own body. But he had witnessed all this without really taking part. By a concerned question he could have redeemed the king and the land, but instead he had followed the advice of his teacher. He was worried about his honor as a knight. He did not want to ask unnecessary questions and thus he remained silent in the face of the miracles and the suffering.

The sword, as a gift from the king, was a call to speak and act. It is a symbol of the power of speech and decision. To free the king of his suffering demanded a question from the heart. Only through compassion from an innocent man could the life-giving force of the Grail heal the king and his land. Chrestien de Troyes called the bleeding lance 'la lance qui saigne' — the lance that heals.

In Wolfram von Eschenbach's version the lance is put into the king's wound to extract the poisons and to diminish the suffering. In another legend Sir Galahad touches the king's wounds with the blood that emerges from the lance. The lance is the cause of his injury — and at the same time it is the remedy for healing. It is a symbol of consciousness. That which injures can also heal if the suffering is conscious.

For the Alchemists, as for many tribal cultures, blood is the seat of the soul. It is a symbol of the force of life and consciousness. When Odysseus enters into Hades the souls of the dead drink sacrificial blood to regain consciousness. Blood has the power to redeem, and in the Christian Eucharist people experience the redeeming power of Christ's blood and body.

A wound that is full of life and bleeds can heal. When suffering is made conscious it changes its character. It becomes part of a personal development. Unlived suffering can make a person hard. The wounds that bleed often stagnate in chronic conditions. When, in the temple of Apollo, the wounded Telephos asked for advice to heal his wounds, the oracle answered: 'That which wounds will

The suffering Grail King and the Lance (illustration for Le Roman du Saint Graal *from John Matthews:* The Grail. The Search for Eternity, *London, Thames & Hudson, 1981).*

also heal!' He thus set out to find Achilles, who wounded him in the battle for Troy. Only Achilles could heal his wounds.

Psychoanalysis — and Homeopathy as well — are based on a related principle. Samuel Hahneman, the founder of homeopathy, assumed that like can be healed with like. Along parallel lines, Sigmund Freud assumed that at the root of every symptom lay an uncompleted inner process. Through analysis he tried to help people to return to these uncompleted experiences in order to make them fully conscious. Using Freud's assumptions Arthur Janov (the founder of Primal Therapy) and others claimed that at the bottom of each symptom lay an unsuffered hurt. In contrast to Freud, Janov believed that it was not enough to bring these incomplete experiences in to consciousness. He claimed that in order to heal it was necessary to actually re-live the hurt from childhood once again.

When a person opens up to the unfelt hurt from childhood and becomes conscious of it, his wounds can bleed. The processes of life that had stagnated in chronic conditions can then flow again, and the wounds can heal. Faced with suffering, Parzival had remained an observer. As the king's suffering was to continue in stagnation, his journey too had become a journey of suffering. The king's wound and the starving of the land had now become his own wound.

Often the beginning of an initiation is marked by an injury. The limits of consciousness have to be wounded before something new can emerge. If a person chooses to live consciously through these injuries, they can be transformed into a journey. His wounds then become an important step in an inner development. They become Sacred Wounds.

In a Guided Exercise you can discover the dimension of a Sacred Would in the context of your own life. You will need a large sheet of paper and crayons or colored pencils. Find a place where you are undisturbed and think about a wounding that played an important part in your life, a wounding that might have influenced the direction of your own life's journey. This might be an experience from childhood; it could also be a physical injury or maybe separation from someone you loved.

Draw an expression of this wounding on the paper. This picture is an expression of your feelings and experiences, it is a part of a vital process (and not a piece of art to be judged). While you draw the image a partner — or this text — will ask you a question. It is the question that Parzival failed to ask in the Grail Castle:

> *'What ails thee? Tell me about your wounding.*
> *What did you feel?'*

Take time to answer these questions, give yourself the space to become fully conscious of what happened.

The picture that emerges in this process is a symbol of a Sacred Wound. Take time to look at this picture when you have finished drawing, and then begin to tell a fantasy that commences with your own wounding. You might choose to write this story down if you are alone and without a partner. Like a fairy tale, you are telling the story of a journey, but the hero of this story is not you as you usually are. It might be a prince or a princess, or maybe an animal or a fairy. Begin by just watching your picture, and let the story then emerge through spontaneous ideas. The pattern of the 'Hero's Journey' can be a help in this process.

As you meet your problems and injuries on a mythological level through the images of a story, it is possible to transcend habitual patterns of experience. The Sacred Wound is a very deep injury. It is a challenge to transform problems into a personal journey.

It is a big undertaking to accept this kind of a challenge. If we accept our injuries or problems as part of our inner development, we can leave the role of victim and take responsibility for our own journey. This is a big step, and it often seems much easier to remain as victim and blame others — our parents for instance — for our suffering. Sometimes this step is so great that we refuse to take it. It might then require many deviations and crises, where we meet the hidden, dark sides of ourselves, until the experience of our personal journey becomes so strong that we are ready to enter consciously into it.

Parzival, too, was at first not ready to accept the challenge of a sacred wound with all its consequences. Only through the encounter with his own shadow was he able to transform the Grail wound into a journey of personal development.

Parzival had ridden for a long time. At night, he met a woman who was riding on an old nag through the forest. Her horse's saddle had broken and instead of reins she held rough ropes in her hands. Her clothes were torn into rags. When Parzival came closer the woman recognised him. Tears ran down her face: 'I have seen you once before,' she said, 'and it brought great suffering to me. It is because of you that I am wearing these clothes and riding this miserable horse.'

Parzival did not understand and offered her his coat, then recognized her as the Duchess Jeschute whose ring he had taken long ago. In the same moment, he saw Duke Orilus galloping, lance raised, towards him. In contrast with Jeschute's poor clothes, the Duke was dressed in silk. His helmet featured the image of a dragon whose eyes were made of glittering rubies. His shield and armour radiated many colors.

Parzival was ready for battle, and the two men clashed with full force. The Duke still believed that his wife had been unfaithful, and in his battle with Parzival he gave vent to his full anger. They hit each other with lances and swords. Horses and knights were covered with sweat and the chain of their armour burst under the force of their blows. In the end, Parzival pulled the Duke from his saddle. He pressed him so violently against a tree that Orilus had to beg for his life. He promised his land and the land of his brother, but Parzival asked him to make peace with Jeschute. He also ordered Orilus to ride to the court of King Arthur in order to offer his services to Lady Cunneware.

Parzival accompanied Orilus and Jeschute to a hermit's hut where, in front of an altar, he swore the innocence of the Duchess and returned the ring that he had once taken. With love, Orilus and Jeschute were reconciled. On continuing their journey they found King Arthur with his court in a camp of many beautiful tents. Kingrun and Clamide had told him of the deeds of the Red Knight, and the king had set off to find this knight and to invite him into the circle of the Round Table.

Parzival, however, continued his journey across the land. No path seemed to lead him back to the Grail Castle. In his heart, he longed for security. Again and again, he saw the image of his mother lying unconscious on the bridge of Soltane. He longed for Condwiramurs, but no path led him back to her. Finally he wanted to ride to King Arthur's court.

It was bitterly cold, and although it was already Pentecost, snow fell during the night. When Parzival awoke in the early hours of the morning, he found a tame falcon who had joined him in the night. When Parzival continued his journey, the tame bird followed him. In the pale light of the morning, Parzival saw a flock of wild geese whose chatter echoed through the silence of the forest. Like a flash of lightning, the falcon struck a goose with his sharp claws. The goose escaped, but three drops of blood fell onto the snow. When Parzival reached the scene, he began to stare at the red blood on the snow. As in a dream the image of Condwiramurs came forward. Everything around him seemed to disappear and he was filled by her being.

The tame bird was a hunting falcon who had escaped from King Arthurs' court. When the king's men left the camp to search for the falcon, they found the Red Knight on his horse in a deep trance, staring at the drops of blood in the snow. They called out to him, but Parzival did not move. Only when a knight threatened him with his lance did Parzival pull his horse to the side. He pushed the knight from his horse and returned to gaze on the drops of red blood in the snow. Again he fell into a dream of love.

Even when the king's seneschal challenged him to a fight, Parzival remained aloof and motionless. When the seneschal's lance hit his shield, however, Parzival forgot the images and hit his opponent with such force that the guardian of the court fell to the ground. Parzival seemed hardly to notice this and again he began to stare at the blood on the snow. Finally the young knight, Gawain, came to him. He was unarmed, and as he was familiar with the power of love he knew that he could not reach this knight in his enchanted state by force of arms. Carefully, he covered the drops of blood with his coat and Parzival painfully let go of his images. Only now, he noticed the young and sympathetic knight who greeted him in a friendly manner.

Gawain told Parzival of King Arthur's camp nearby, and invited him to follow. Parzival's hurt and his desperation now seemed to dissolve: King Arthur and the Knights of the Round Table were here! Why should be care any longer about the sad figures in the castle of Munsalvasche, and the pain of his cousin who had rejected him? Finally, he was among people again. The understanding and sympathy of the young knight warmed him. The sun had melted the snow, and when he entered the king's camp it seemed as if a shadow had left his heart.

King Arthur was excited about the arrival of the knight and received him with great honor. The Lady Cunneware greeted him with a kiss. In his honor the Round Table gathered for a feast, and all the knights praised his fame and his deeds. Parzival was now admitted into the circle of the Round Table, and even the Queen forgave him for the death of Sir Ither. The celebrations lasted for three days, and Parzival's beauty and his courage shone among the knights and their ladies.

On the third day, however, a strange figure on a mule

entered the festive circle of the knights. When she arrived all laughter stopped, there was total silence. She looked awful: she was human and animal at the same time; she wore a long coat of blue silk and a hat with a peacock feather and a lining of golden silk. Her nose was like that of a dog. Boar teeth jutted out of her mouth. She had bushy eyebrows and her hair was braided, black and brittle. On her chest she had a hump and her back was deformed. Her fingers were long like those of a lion, and in her hands, like claws, she held a whip with silk strings. This was Cundry, the sorceress. She was educated in all languages. She knew astrology, logic and geometry. Slowly she rode through the silent crowd, then she turned to King Arthur, who sat at the end of the table. Her face was marked by deep pain, and in a bitter voice she told the king and the round Table that they had lost all honor by allowing a person without honor into their midst. Then Cundry turned to Parzival:

> 'Shame on you, Sir Parzival,' she said, 'you are the reason I cannot greet the king and his knights. I am horrified by your beauty and your faultlessness. I may seem ugly to you, but inside you are much uglier than I am. Tell me, Sir Parzival, why you did not free the king from his suffering when he sat with you, helpless and in agony? Oh, you showed no mercy. You saw the suffering and the lance from which the blood flowed, and you still remained in silence. You took the sword, but remained indifferent when they carried the Grail in front of you. If only you had spoken to redeem the king and his land.'

Cundry was an image of sorrow. Tears streamed down her face, and again and again she cursed Parzival's silence. Before she left the Round Table then, she told the knights of a mysterious castle where Klingsor, the magician, kept four-hundred women and four queens prisoner. Gawain's sisters had been taken there, too, and Cundry challenged the Round Table to find the mysterious castle and to free the women. Without farewell, but in tears, the messenger of the Grail rode off on her mule. Again and again, she exclaimed: 'Oh, Munsalvasche, place of deep sorrow, nobody can comfort you.' The knights listened in silence to her cries, and Cundry disappeared into the forest.

When Cunneware saw her proud knight so humiliated she wept. Parzival was in deep dismay. The suffering of the Grail King had now become his own suffering. When the knights tried to console him, he thanked them for their words, but he felt so miserable and their words could not take away his pain:

> 'You have heard the accusations of the Grail messenger and I cannot stay with you. There will be no peace for me until I have found the Grail Castle again. I will no longer stay for two nights under the same roof, and no path shall be untried until I have found the Grail again to redeem the king and his land.'

When Parzival departed, Gawain wished the blessings of God upon his friend. Parzival, however, exclaimed in despair:

> 'Oh, what is God? I have served him all my life and I hoped to be rewarded. Now I will not serve him any more and if he hates me I can bear it. I hope that the love of women is a better protection than trust in God.'

Parzival had lost both his fame as a knight and his faith. He had nothing left to cling to. Now he was ready to meet the challenge of a Sacred Wound and to find his own way. Before he left the Round Table, he arranged the marriage between Cunneware and Clamide. Then he rode off.

Cundry is a messenger of the Grail. In her ugliness, she mirrors Parzival's dark, still unconscious side. Now that he is a knight of the Round Table, she appears, and with her animal claws points to his dark shadow: 'I might seem horrible to you,' she says, 'but you are much uglier than I.' She accuses him because, in spite of his fame, Parzival has failed at a deeper level.

Cundry is a messenger of wholeness. In her ugly appearance she embodies parts of us that we do not want to acknowledge, the parts that we banish from our conscious awareness. She confronts us with our shadow.

When we believe we are perfect, Cundry appears on her ragged mule. If we believe ourselves to be spiritually aware, meditating in a perfect lotus position, she will ride into our temple. If, on our spiritual journey, we have excluded a part of ourselves, it may be that she will appear one day in her ugliness. 'You want to be enlightened,' she might say, 'but there is a knot in your stomach that holds you and keeps you from being fully alive.' Hopefully, we will then listen to her because Cundry is a great teacher. She points to the parts of us that we need to integrate to become whole.

At times, she might ride on her mule into therapy and encounter groups. Where we deal exclusively with our own problems and feelings, she almost seems to mock us. Whenever she enters the room, everything becomes silent aandwith her bony fingers she may point at us: 'For years now, you have searched to find yourself. You have become more sensitive, more open, more honest and creative, but to see you causes me great pain. Don't you see how the world around you is destroyed and the earth is poisoned? Don't you see that there are no more fish in the rivers, that the trees are dying and your environment slowly turns to desert? And do you believe that you have no part in this?'

Initially, we might be shocked, because Cundry is incredibly ugly. Her appearance might seem absolutely inappropriate. To see her pain might silence us, however. If we listen inwardly, we might then realize that she is a messenger who can lead us to realms that we are not yet aware of.

In her sorrow, Cundry links the inner and outer worlds. She laments the pain of the king and, at the same time, the suffering of the land. From her point of view, our own suffering cannot be separated from the suffering of the land. Her pain is the hurt in us. It is the pain of Mother Earth, the dying trees, the hungry and desperate. Cundry embodies the emergence of an awareness that we are one with all human beings, with plants, animals and our Mother Earth. She shows us that our problems are a part of a whole whose balance is upset. As a messenger of wholeness she confronts us with the limitations of our consciousness, and she calls us to go beyond these limitations.

Cundry is an uninvited goddess who has turned ugly in exile. In a seminar, I once dramatized this encounter with Cundry, as a confrontation with our own shadows. As in drama, we have developed Cundry's role as a personal figure and have entered into a dialogue with her.

Cundry is a different character for each person. As an embodiment of our own shadow, she shows us in her ugliness the still unconscious, unlived parts of ourselves. These parts are often so unpleasant and threatening that we would rather not acknowledge them. Whatever we disown and ban from our awareness, though, we usually meet in our contact with other people — as projections.

When we discover the traits of our own shadow in another person, we often react strongly. We might be outraged or shocked; we might feel disgusted, our pulse might rise and often we become intolerant or furious. A strong reaction like this can show us that parts of ourselves need to be acknowledged and redeemed. To discover Cundry's being within ourselves, we have looked at our own shadow. In a game, we have imitated the traits and behaviour of people we strongly disliked, people whose presence evoked a strong reaction in us. In dance, we have found positions and movement that expressed their way of being. In doing so, we have experienced the qualities that we disliked so much within ourselves. Through this encounter with our own shadow, we began to develop Cundry's character.

We can also discover Cundry's being through our bodies. The unaccepted forces of life, the unfulfilled desires and the impulses that we have suppressed have become 'embodied' in the course of time. We can find them in the posture of our body, in the tension of our muscles and sometimes in chronic illnesses.

At some point in time, this muscular tension might

have been a useful reaction to protect us from the intensity of experiences which we could not live with. With the help of the body, we have thus banished the pain from our awareness. But what originally might have helped to protect us has, in time, often become autonomous — a way of being that finds its expression in our body.

To develop Cundry's character, we dramatized these tensions in the body. Lying down on a flat surface, we tried to relax completely. In a guided journey, we touched each part of the body with awareness. Wherever we found it difficult to relax and let go, we then consciously increased the tension. If the muscles in our face were tense, we intensified this tension. If the shoulders were hunched, we increased this tendency. We intensified the tension in the neck, the arms, the legs, in our back and stomach. By following the tension in our muscles and increasing it, we found ugly and grotesque postures and movements in our body — the character of Cundry came alive.

As Cundry, we then began to move. Each person entered our circle in the role of Cundry. The circle represented an everyday situation in our lives. This might have been in a workplace, a library, a classroom, a stage or an office. It might be a children's room, or, simply, home. As Cundry, each person in turn entered the circle and began a dialogue with his normal self, which was represented by an empty chair. As a messenger of a deeper sphere, he or she began to speak ...

What we said was unprepared. It was called from an inner depth through the position of our bodies. For many of us, our speech was initially an accusation. Cundry, however, is a messenger of wholeness. She is never hateful nor destructive. Her pain is a challenge. It is the hurt of everything that we suppress, a deep longing for redemption.

This encounter with Cundry was different for each one of us. In role play with an empty chair, we dramatized a dialogue between our normal selves and this character from the depth of the soul. It was a lively and fascinating process, a very direct encounter with yet unlived forces in ourselves that we could thus call on and integrate. You can experience this encounter with Cundry alone or, even better, in a group of friends.

To find the traits of your Cundry you can imitate people who produce a strong reaction in you, people whose presence might make you feel uptight, angry or depressed.

To find a bodily posture for your Cundry, intensify all tensions in your body. Begin by lying on a flat surface. Relax, and become aware of the parts where it is difficult to let go. Let your awareness touch every part of your body. Then, let yourself intensify any tensions in your muscles. By following these tensions and exaggerating them, you can find a posture for your Cundry.

You can dramatize the encounter with Cundry in words and in dialogue with an empty chair. You can also just imagine such an encounter. The posture of your body is of vital importance, however. As the messenger of a deeper sphere you will then meet your normal self in an everyday situation. As Cundry you then begin to talk ...

In role play with an empty chair, you can also switch the roles. In this way you can answer Cundry from your normal point of view. You can ask questions and enter into a dialogue. In the course of your encounter you may come to new insights. Cundry is a dramatization of a deeper level of yourself. She can lead you to still unexplored parts of your self.

Chapter 11
Gawain

With Parzival's departure from the Round Table the story changes. It now tells of the adventures of Sir Gawain.

When Parzival left, a heavily armed knight, Prince Kingrimursel, appeared in the midst of the confusion at the Round Table. He accused Gawain of killing his master and challenged him to a battle in Schanpfanzun in fourteen days' time. Thus Gawain, too, left the Round Table to fight with Kingrimursel and to free the women from the castle of a magician.

After several days, Gawain came upon the army of King Meljanz. The mules and wagons of the king's knights were followed by a bunch of tramps and prostitutes. With this colorful army the young king went into battle against his stepfather, Count Lippaut. King Meljanz was a strong and courageous man. He was unrestrained and impulsive, and it was said that he violated women whenever he fancied. However, when he fell in love with Obie, the daughter of his stepfather, she ridiculed him: she laughed at his love and recommended he first prove himself in battle. To break her pride, Meljanz had now turned against her town.

On the first day, her father's army had suffered great losses, and that night Obie's younger sister, Obilot, came to the town gate and asked Gawain for his services. Little Obilot was determined to make him her knight. 'Even if we have different names, we are in reality inseparable, and connected to each other,' she said, 'If you wish, I will give you all the love in my heart and you will be both man and woman at the same time.'

Gawain listened with surprise to the little girl. She was much too young to be courted, but as Parzival had recommended that he trust women more than God, Gawain promised to fight in her service. To protect him, Obilot gave him a sleeve of her dress. Gawain pinned the silk to his shield and in battle he beat King Meljanz. When he returned to the town, little Obilot took her knight into her arms, and only with tears did she let him leave again. Gawain demanded that Meljanz be reconciled with the Count and his daughter Obie, then he continued on his way to Schanpfanzun.

He rode for many days, and when he came close to the town he met King Vergulacht on an Arabian battle horse. Whilst hunting, the king had entered a swamp. His clothes were utterly wet and muddy and he asked Gawain to ride to the town to his sister, Antikonie.

When Gawain entered the palace he was surprised by the extraordinary beauty of King Vergulacht's sister. Antikonie, who was well aware of her beauty, took Gawain by the hand and led him into her room. To welcome her guest, she kissed the young knight, but this soon turned into an embrace and a long kiss, which was not usual on such an occasion. Gawain had not expected this kind of welcome, and as both seemed skilled in the art of courtly love, the knights and ladies soon withdrew and left the pair alone. In the rituals of this ancient game, he made his plea and she playfully rejected him. Wolfram describes the scene in much detail: when Gawain let his hand slide under her coat and touched her hip, his desire became intolerable. Passionately they desired each other: '*... daz da nach was ein dinc geschehen, hetenz ubel Ougen niht ersehen*' ('... that something would have happened if malicious eyes had not seen them').

A knight with white hair had opened the door, and upon recognizing Gawain he exclaimed: 'Was it not enough to kill our master? Do you want to rape his daughter as well?' Armed knights and merchants stormed into the hall, and Gawain and Antikonie fled through a stairway into the tower. He was completely unarmed, and with an iron bar he defended the door against the crowd. Finally, Antikonie found a huge chess set with which her knight defended her. She threw the heavy pieces into the crowd, and whoever was hit sank to the ground. Her beauty seemed to give Gawain great strength, but in spite of it his position was rather bleak. It did not improve when King Vergulacht stepped into the hall and encouraged his men to fight. He himself, dressed in full armour, took part in this uneven battle.

At last Kingrimursel appeared in the hall. It was he who had challenged Gawain to come to Schanpfanzun and had promised him clear passage. When he saw that his word had been broken, he fought on the side of Gawain and Antikonie and eventually the men retreated. Antikonie was furious with her brother, King Vergulacht, but the king retreated to decide on Gawain's fate.

Some days earlier, King Vergulacht had been beaten in a fight with a knight in red armour. As the loser, he had to promise to find the Grail, and if he was unable to do so he must enter the service of the Queen of Pelrapeire. To free himself from this task he decided to pass it on to his prisoner, and Gawain left Antikonie and the town of Schanpfanzun.

Chapter 12
Trevrizent

While Gawain's adventures are being recounted, Parzival's journey remains obscure. Again and again he appears on the edge of the story, so that it seems as if their paths are mysteriously connected, as if they embodied two aspects of a common journey.

The story now turns to Parzival who, restless and despairing, rides through the world. He has not stayed for two nights in the same place. He has fought many battles but does not seem to have come closer to the Grail.

One day, Parzival rode through a dark forest and came to the house of Sigune. By now she had put her lover into a coffin and lived in solitude and great despair. When Parzival looked through the window of her hut, he found her absorbed in prayer. She wore a simple shirt and a grey skirt, her face was gaunt and her skin was pale. Despair had aged Sigune and Parzival did not recognize her. When Sigune saw the knight, she offered him a seat in front of her hut. She herself did not leave the house. Parzival could not understand how this woman spent her life with a dead person. On being questioned, Sigune told him of her love for the dead Schionatulander, who had lost his life in a battle with Duke Orilus. She wanted to stay with her lover until her own death united them.

When Parzival and Sigune finally recognised one another, she asked him about his life. Parzival sighed:

> 'I have no more joy in life because the search for the Grail is a torture. Years ago, I left the land where I was king. I have left behind a woman that I still love with all

my heart. The longing for her is painful. In my heart, I long for the Grail.'

Sigune listened to him in silence and then told him that Cundry had just been with her. Once a week the sorceress came to bring her food from the Grail. Sigune led Parzival to a spring that came from a rock and showed him the hoof-prints of Cundry's mule. Immediately Parzival set off on his way, but when the tracks led into a river bed he lost them.

Parzival, however, had already entered the realm of the Grail, and soon met a knight in shining armour. His head was uncovered and in his hand he held a silver helmet with silken strings. 'Munsalvasche is not used to people riding so close,' he called out angrily, and rode directly towards Parzival, 'Whoever enters this land has to fight a dangerous battle and make a sacrifice. Outside this forest they call the sacrifice Death.'

Furiously, Parzival watched the knight, then they charged towards each other. Through the power of their collision the knight of Munsalvasche was thrown from his horse and fell into a deep ravine, and Parzival was unable to hold his own horse. It fell into the abyss and crashed onto the rocks. With both hands Parzival clung to the branches of a tree. Below him, he saw his dead horse, but when he reached the edge of the ravine, he discovered the horse of his opponent, wearing a saddle blanket from Munsalvasche with a white dove embroidered upon it. Parzival mounted the horse, took the reins and rode off.

Again, many weeks passed and Parzival was still riding through the forest where he had met the knight of the Grail. But no traces led him back to Munsalvasche. It had started to grow cold, and one day there was fresh snow. On this morning Parzival met a group of pilgrims. Their clothes were grey and with bare feet they walked through the snow. An old knight was followed by servants with dogs, and horses loaded with baggage. The old knight was horrified to see Parzival and asked him why he was riding on this sacred day in armour and with weapons. But Parzival did not know the days, he did not know when the year had started, and every day was the same.

'Today is Good Friday,' said the old man, and he told him of Jesus Christ who was crucified on this day. 'If you are not a heathen, then come with us.' The knight was on his way to a holy man who lived close by. Every year he took a pilgrimage there to pray and confess. The strange pilgrims reminded Parzival of a time when he, too, believed in God and served him. But since then he had turned away from God, there were no more holy days; every day was the same as the one before. The noble knights asked him again to join the pilgrimage to the house of the pious hermit. Parzival hesitated for a moment, and then refused.

As he continued his journey, his thoughts wandered to the words of the pilgrims. Parzival longed for the feeling of belonging. These pilgrims knew where they belonged, they knew what was good and what was bad, but Parzival could not follow their path. Lost in thought, he loosened the reins of his horse and began to canter. He listened to the sound of the hooves on the fresh snow, and when he next looked up he found himself in front of the hut of a hermit.

Trevrizent was a pious man. He was not a priest but his life was one single prayer. He ate neither meat nor fish, and to unite with God he fasted the whole week. Trevrizent, too, was surprised to find an armed knight on this day. He asked his guest to take off the heavy armour and to join him at the fire. Parzival was tired. He felt cold, and with pleasure he accepted the invitation. Later, when he sat at the fire and looked into the clear eyes of the old man, he began to feel his full misery. 'Oh, give me your advice,' he said, 'I am a man burdened with sin.' The hermit lit a candle and Parzival began to tell his story.

He told him how he had left King Arthur's Round Table to find the Grail, and how for years he had ridden through an inner desert. The old man listened to him in silence. By the light of the candles, Parzival then recognised the altar in front of which he had once sworn the innocence of Duchess Jeschute. He remembered that at the time he had thoughtlessly taken a colored lance with him. With this lance, he had broken the bones of the king's seneschal when he tried to awaken him from his trance at the blood in the snow.

The hermit had discovered the loss of the lance and entered it into his diary. It was four and a half years and three days since Parzival had left the hermit's house. On this day — it was the day of Saint Michael — Parzival had left the Grail Castle. Since then he had been wandering without hope through the world.

> 'All I sought was battle. I am deeply resentful of God, since he stands godfather to my troubles. He has lifted them up too high, while my happiness is buried alive. If only God's power would succour me, how firm my happiness would be, which now sinks into sorrow's silt! If my manly heart is wounded — can it be whole when Sorrow sets her thorny crown on glory won by deeds of arms from formidable foes?'

Trevrizent listened to him in silence, and then taught him about the loyalty of God. He told him the story of Cain and Abel:

> 'The earth was Adam's mother. She had borne him as a virgin and nourished him with her fruits. Adam's son, Cain, killed his brother, Abel, and when his blood touched the earth she had lost her innocence. From now on, there was war among people on earth.
>
> To free humanity from discord and sin, God's Son then took human form. He too was born of a virgin. This was God's loyalty. As Christ lived through death, humanity was redeemed of its sorrows and its sins.'

Parzival listened in silence and thanked the old man for his words. God's loyalty, however, was strange to him.

Trevrizent told him also of the secrets of the Grail. He told him of the community of the Grail whose nourishment came from a miraculous stone. (In some legends, as for example in Chrestien de Troyes' *Perceval*, the Grail is a chalice.)

> 'They live from a stone whose essence is most pure ... By virtue of this stone the Phoenix is burned to ashes, in which he is reborn ...' Furthermore, however ill a mortal may be, from the day on which he sees the stone he cannot die for that week ...'

The hermit told him that once a year, on Good Friday, a dove came from the sky to put a consecrated wafer on the stone through which the magic force of the Grail was renewed. He told Parzival that the Grail can never be fought for, that it can only be found by those who are called to it.

Trevrizent told him also about his brother, Anfortas. After the death of his father, Frimutel, Anfortas had become the new king of the Grail. He was still young and fell in love with a woman. In her service, he broke the laws of the Grail. As a knight, he travelled through many countries and one day was injured on the testicle by a heathen spear. Trevrizent had, himself, once been a knight. When he saw the pain of Anfortas, however, he prayed to God. To relieve his brother's suffering he promised to give up his life as a knight, and since that day had lived in solitude and prayer. But Anfortas' wound did not heal. It was full of pus and the king was in deep pain. No remedy seemed to help. His land began to dry up and turned to desert.

One day, there was a writing on the Grail which said that a knight would come, and if this knight were to ask the king out of compassion about the nature of his suffering, Anfortas could be healed. When the young knight appeared, however, he failed to ask the redeeming question. He remained in silence in the face of the king's suffering. Burdened with sin, he left the Grail Castle and the suffering of the king continued.

Parzival listened in silence. When Trevrizent asked him about his ancestry, he told him of Gahmuret and Herzeloyde. Like Anfortas, Trevrizent was a brother of Herzeloyde and Parzival's uncle. He lamented the death of his sister:

> 'No sooner had you left your mother than she died — that was how she was rewarded for her love. You were the beast she suckled, the dragon that flew away from her. It had come upon her as she slept, sweet lady, before giving birth to you ...'

To find his way, Parzival had to leave the world of his mother, but in doing so he had caused her death. Now, in his conversation with Trevrizent, the hurt of her loss was revived in him again.

The hermit led Parzival outside to find roots and grass for his horse. When Trevrizent saw the white dove on the horse's blanket, he lamented the great suffering of his brother. Parzival was undecided for a moment. In silence he looked at the old man who was so deeply touched by the pain of his brother. Finally, he said: 'I was the knight who came to Munsalvasche. It was I who saw the suffering of the king and did not ask any questions.' Trevrizent looked at him perplexed, but he did not curse him; he regretted his misfortune. 'God has not left you,' he said, 'And in His Name I am here to help.'

Trevrizent was a priest outside the church. Wolfram calls him a 'good man' and he might have been one of the 'bon hommes', a priest in the community of Cathars. The centre of his belief was the eternal cycle of life, death and rebirth — the mystery of the phoenix who burns to ash to unfold in new life again. When Parzival entered his hut, he did not say Mass for him; instead, he listened to him, and then told him of Christ who redeemed humanity through His own death. We have come to know this circle of life, death and rebirth in symbolic form as the 'Hero's Journey'. This cycle is a part of the mysteries and myths of many times and cultures. There is Persephone's descent and return from the underworld, or the myth of Isis and Osiris and the journey of the Sumerian goddess, Innana, who lived through death and returned as an initiate into life. The rhythms of life are mirrored in this cycle, the pattern of inhaling and exhaling, of day and night and the changes of the seasons.

Parzival began to realize that he stood outside this

cycle. He did not know when the year had started and aimlessly he rode through the land. On Good Friday he had entered the hut of his uncle. This was the day of Christ's death, and people celebrate this day as the lowest point in a sacred cycle of life, death and rebirth. In the course of their conversation, Parzival began to see himself within the cycle again. The mystery of Good Friday corresponded to his inner condition. Once again, the old man reminded Parzival of his mother's death, of his encounter with the Red Knight and the suffering of Anfortas. It was as if Trevrizent led Parzival once again into the underworld of the soul. Then he gave him courage because each death is followed by new growth.

Within the realm of the Grail, this cycle of life was stagnant. The king could neither live nor die. Lifelessly, he was ailing, and his land could bear no more fruit. In the old tribal cultures, the health of the king was seen as directly linked with the well-being of the land. The leader was the life centre of the people. In a sense, he embodied the fertility of the land and the health of the people. When their leader was old and sick, he was ritually killed so the force of life could unfold in his successor.

Because of the power of the Grail, Anfortas was unable to die. When Parzival visited the Grail Castle, fresh snow had fallen in the middle of summer. Saturn had reached its highest position and the suffering of the king was worse than ever. His body was colder than ice, and the 'inner frost' caused him great pain. Under the forces of Saturn, the processes of life had stagnated. Parzival, who was called to release this stagnation through a question from the heart, failed to ask the redeeming question.

For the people of the Middle Ages, Saturn was a planet of death and stagnation. In modern astrology, however, Saturn is a planet of consciousness as well as death. In this sense the king's wound is a call for consciousness, a sacred wound, and a manifestation of yet unlived forces in the world of the Grail. To heal, these forces have to be made conscious and lived.

But what are the forces that were manifested in

Anfortas' wound? What *was* the origin of the suffering?

In a prologue to Chrestien de Troyes' *Perceval*, in the 'Elucidations', the land of the Grail is described in its original condition: it was rich and fertile. In the hills from where the springs flowed, lived young maidens who gave freely of their wealth. If a wanderer approached these springs, the maidens came from the earth. From a golden bowl they gave nourishment to the hungry. Whatever people wished for, they found at the spring with the beautiful maidens.

One day, however, King Amangon did violence to the maidens and seized the golden bowl. From then on, the land became impoverished. The springs ceased to flow, the trees bore no more leaves. Never again did the girls appear from the caves to give their wealth to the people:

> 'The land was dead and a desert ... [and] so they lost the voices of the wells ... and the maidens who were in them.'
>
> (E.C. Whitmont, *Return of the Goddess*)

Violation of the maidens caused the land to turn to desert. When the king stole their bowl he had turned against the feminine as well as against nature.

The realm of the Grail is a masculine one. By his love for a women Anfortas had disregarded the laws of the Grail and was wounded in the testicle during a battle. In his wound are embodied the forces of the feminine that the Grail world needs to become whole; through his wound they enter into the consciousness of that masculine world. To heal the king and the land, the forces of the feminine have to be redeemed and integrated. Only then can the circle of life become strong again. When the masculine is united with the feminine, the springs can flow again.

In many tales of King Arthur's knights, it is Gawain who enters into this union with the world of the feminine. In mysterious realms of the beyond, he meets the women of his soul. He defends the right of little Obilot, he fights with Antikonie for his life, and he will free the imprisoned women from the hands of a magician. His adventures lead him beyond the 'Minne', the courtly love and admiration of women of the Middle Ages. By redeeming the feminine, and by allowing himself to be personally touched by it, Gawain becomes a mediator between the worlds. A story from the fourteenth century may illustrate this task.

Chapter 13
Sir Gawain and the Green Knight

Once when King Arthur was gathered with knights and ladies at the Round Table to celebrate the New Year, a giant knight on a green horse suddenly entered the hall. Green was his armour and shield, and even his face was pale and green. In his hands he held a branch of holly and an old battle-axe whose blade was shining green. The Green Knight greeted the king and challenged the knights of the Round Table to play a game with him: a knight was to decapitate him with a single blow of his axe. On New Year's Day of the following year, the same knight was to visit him in a green chapel, where the Green Knight would then decapitate him with a stroke of his axe. Nobody was interested in such a game and a sullen silence spread amongst the knights. When King Arthur rose, however, to save the honor of the Round Table, Gawain declared himself ready to meet the challenge of the Green Knight.

The Green Knight slowly descended from his horse. He took off his helmet and gave Gawain the heavy axe. Gawain lifted the axe and, with a strong blow, decapitated the Green Knight. His head fell to the ground and rolled a little way. The Green Knight, however, slowly rose, took the axe and his head under his arm, and mounted his horse. Blood was dripping and his lips were moving as his head bid farewell to Gawain and the Round Table. In a year's time, he was to expect Gawain in the Green Chapel.

At the end of the year, Gawain set out on his journey. It was a sad departure because nobody believed that he would return from this adventure. He rode for many days and everywhere he asked for the Chapel of the Green Knight, but no-one had ever heard of it.

On Christmas Eve, Gawain discovered a castle in the middle of a forest. A knight lived here with his young wife and an old matron. When Gawain asked for the green chapel, the knight told him that it was only a few miles away. He invited Gawain to stay with him until the end of the year. Gawain, who was happy to have found the way to the chapel, accepted the invitation. During the daytime the knight went hunting, and at night the men sat by the fire drinking and telling each other stories.

One night, the host asked his guest to play a game. For three days, Gawain was to stay with the women in the house. He himself was to go hunting, and at night he would bring the spoils of his hunt and exchange them for the things Gawain had experienced during his day in the castle. They laughed about the uneven exchange, and when the fire died they went to bed.

At the break of dawn the knight went hunting. Half asleep, Gawain heard the barking of the dogs and the sounding of horns. Then it became quiet in the castle, and when Gawain opened his eyes they alighted on the knight's young wife. She had opened the curtain to his bed and began a friendly conversation. Her eyes were glowing and her voice was gentle and full. When Gawain saw the beauty of the young woman, his heart was set on fire, but as a knight he felt obligated to his host. He merely kissed her lightly on her cheek. At night when the knight returned from the hunt, he brought the spoils to his guest. Gawain, too, gave his host what he had experienced — he kissed him quickly on the cheek.

The next day saw a repeat of the same game. When the knight left the castle, the young woman entered the room of her guest and opened the curtain to his bed. When Gawain awoke, she wanted more than just a kiss. Gawain, too, desired her with all his heart, but, as a knight, he felt obligated to his host. Without embarrassing her, he withdrew from the embrace. When, at night, the knight brought him the spoils of the hunt, Gawain gave him the experiences of the day. He kissed him twice on the cheek.

When the lady of the knight entered Gawain's room on the third day, she was determined not to be satisfied with soft words and a quick kiss. Gawain's reputation was not only that of a knight but also that of a lover, and her desire for him was great. With shaking hands she opened the curtain to his bed and touched his skin. When Gawain awoke he found himself in an inner turmoil He knew his duties as a knight, but at the same time he desired this young woman with all his being. He knew that these were the last hours of his life, and he would have loved to enjoy life once more in its full richness. On the other hand, however, he had served the ideal of a perfect knight for his whole life. Should he surrender his ideal shortly before his death for an adventure in love?

The young woman was persistent. With all her charm, she tried to seduce him. She begged and beseeched him, and when Gawain did not respond to her desire she was close to tears. Finally, she took a piece of green silk that she wore around her hips. To unite with Gawain, she put it in his hand. 'Take this token of me, it has magic powers. Whoever carries the silk cannot be hurt.' Gawain was doubtful for a moment, but then he closed his hand around the woman's gift. She kissed him three times and then left the room.

In the evening, the knight returned from the hunt. All he had caught during the day was an old fox, and this he gave to his guest. Gawain was embarrassed, and he kissed the young knight three times on his cheek. The green silk, however, he did not mention.

On the last day of the year, Gawain set out on his journey to find the Green Knight. After a few hours he came to a dark ruin that was covered in moss. It was eerie here, and from afar he heard the sounds of an axe being sharpened. He descended from his horse and waited patiently. When the Green Knight finally appeared, the men greeted each other swiftly. Gawain took his helmet off and freed his neck. Slowly he bent forward. When the Green Knight raised the axe, Gawain shuddered and twitched. The Green Knight put the axe aside and called him a coward. Again Gawain bent forward, and when the Green Knight lifted the axe for a second time, he did not move. But the Green Knight did not let the axe fall. Gawain begged him to finish the task, and when the Green Knight raised his axe for the third time it fell upon Gawain. Instead of killing him, however, it merely scratched his neck. When Gawain rose, he recognised the Green Knight as the knight from the castle where he had spent the last days. 'The first two blows were harmless,' said the knight, 'because twice you kept your promise and gave me the kisses of my wife. The third time I hurt you because you did not give me the green silk that my wife gave to you.'

Gawain's adventure is like an initiation in the realm of the feminine. The old matron in the castle was Morgan Le Fay. She was Merlin's lover, and it was from her fairy realm that the Green Knight came to King Arthur on New Year's Day to challenge the Round Table.

Gawain had mastered the masculine world already. He was called the pearl of knighthood. To be initiated, however, he had to leave the world of the masculine: he had to lose his head. Facing death, he entered another realm, and on his journey he met wild animals and mysterious beings:

> 'He met so many marvels in those hills it is difficult to tell a tenth of it — dragons attacked him, and sometimes wolves, and satyrs, and forest trolls, running out of rocks, and bulls, and bears, and ivory tusked boars, and giant ogres leaping crags.'
>
> (Burton Raffael, *Sir Gawain and the Green Knight*)

In the castle of Morgan Le Fay, Gawain found the wife of the Green Knight. Gawain allowed himself to be touched by the feminine. He did not hurt her. At the same time, however, he remained loyal to his masculine ideals. In his inner conflict, the masculine and feminine entered into process. Gawain became a mediator between the world of the knights and the mysterious feminine world of Morgan Le Fay.

In some legends of the Middle Ages, it is Gawain who redeems the Grail — and it seems as if Parzival and Gawain were originally one person. In the Welsh fairy tale, 'Peredur', which is related to the Parzival story, Parzival is called 'Gwri-Gwalt Adwyn' (the Fair Haired One). In the course of time, this name might have been contracted to Gawain. And, like Gwri-Gwalt Adwyn, Gawain is a knight with fair hair. Originally he was a Celtic god of the sun. His power grew with the rising sun, and after the sun had reached its highest point his strength began to decrease again. Because of this, knightly battle games at King Arthur's court always took place when the sun was high.

Gawain was a solar, masculine knight. His path led him into the realm of the feminine. Parzival, however, was a lunar knight. As the son of a widow, he was directly linked to the feminine. His path led him into the masculine world which had stagnated and awaited redemption. Parzival had missed his opportunity to redeem the world of the Grail, and was therefore expelled from it. He was in despair, and it is at this point that we lose sight of him. Wolfram von Eschenbach now tells of Gawain's adventures, and it seems that Gawain took on a part of the task that Parzival could not fulfil.

To redeem the world of the Grail, Parzival had to go through an initiation. This path of initiation is now described in Gawain's adventures. Only when the feminine is redeemed, when the queens and the four-hundred women are freed from the magic castle, will Parzival be able to return to the Grail Castle. The Grail is a symbol of wholeness. It is the stone where opposites become one. In the search for the Grail, the solar-masculine unites with the lunar-feminine. Both realms — the world of the Grail, and the castle of the imprisoned women — were unable to

The union of the masculine and the feminine (William Blake, Victoria & Albert Museum, London).

free themselves; both needed to enter into consciousness and be redeemed.

In the courts of the Middle Ages, the feminine was idealised: in the Minne, the knights courted the ladies. But the world of the courts was totally determined by masculine ideals. The veneration of women was superficial, and it did not take long for it to be changed into its opposite — the medieval witch-hunts. Gawain's task was not the veneration of women in the Minne, but the release of the feminine, the lunar, in his own being. It was an encounter with the still-uninvited goddesses who demanded their release — and, above everything else, their self-determination. Another contemporary story illustrates this well.

While out hunting, King Arthur met a terrible knight who threatened him with his magical powers. This was

Gromar, the knight of the Wicked Goddess Castle. As the king was unarmed Gromar did not kill him, but ordered him to find out within a year what it was that women wished for most. If he succeeded, he would be pardoned; if he failed, he would be killed at the end of the year.

King Arthur travelled with his knights throughout the country. They searched everywhere for the answer to the mysterious knight's question. In the course of time, Arthur found many answers, but none of them seemed to be the right one. When the year came to its close, King Arthur was in anguish. One day, however, in a lonely forest he met a servant of Morgan Le Fay. She was the ugliest woman he had ever seen. Her face was puffed up and red, rotten yellow teeth stuck out of her mouth, her body was deformed and fat. On her back she carried a lute, and she rode on a saddled mule. She greeted Arthur and promptly offered him the answer to his question. For this, however, the king was to marry her to his nephew. 'I may look horrible,,' she said, 'but I am merry. Now go home and talk to your nephew.' When Gawain heard of this strange encounter, he was immediately prepared to save the king and marry the ugly woman.

The answer to the king's question was as follows: 'What women desire above all', said the ugly woman of the forest, 'is their self-determination.' When, at the end of the year, King Arthur gave this answer to the horrible knight, Gromar, his power was broken and he rode angrily away.

Soon after this, the ugly Dame Ragnell appeared in the castle. The king was somewhat ashamed and the queen, too, wished for a quiet wedding for her nephew and the ugly woman. The bride, however, insisted on a wedding in the church and a large celebration in the court. After the Mass, everybody gathered for a great banquet. The knights and ladies then watched with horror as the bride tore the meat from the bone and swallowed it like an animal. After the meal, Dame Ragnell took her husband by the hand and led him to the bridal chamber.

When Gawain was alone with his bride, he shuddered.

In bed, he immediately turned away, but Dame Ragnell reminded him of his marital duties. 'If I were beautiful, you would not turn away from me,' she said, and asked him for a kiss. Gawain hesitated, but then remembered his promise. 'I am your husband,' he said, 'and I will do more than kiss you.' When he turned to her, he found the most beautiful woman he had ever seen. Tenderly he embraced her.

Later in the night, the beautiful woman said to Gawain: 'You have freed me from a wicked spell, but my beauty will only last for half of every day. After that, I will be ugly and foul again. You are to decide if I am to be beautiful by day and ugly by night, or beautiful at night and ugly by day.' It was a difficult choice. Gawain would have liked to avoid embarrassment at the court, but the thought of her ugliness in his bed made him shudder. Finally, he asked her to decide, putting the decision back into her hands — and by giving her self-determination, totally freed her from her ugliness. Now she was beautiful by day and by night.

Chapter 14
The Magic Castle

Gawain's adventures correspond to the lower half of the circle of the Hero's Journey. This is the road of trials, on the other side of the threshold of adventure. It is where a person meets the uninvited gods that call to be redeemed. Like Dame Ragnell, these forces, when still unredeemed, are often ugly. As invited gods, however, they can unfold their power in its true beauty and richness.

The forces a person meets in this part of the journey are different for each individual. While one person may meet his unredeemed sexuality, another may discover unresolved experiences from childhood. Gawain, as a solar hero, had to enter into the feminine, lunar sphere.

Although this road of trials is different for each person, it appears that there is a common thread to this part of the journey. To open a new way of being, a person has to be ready to go beyond the limits of an old, outdated state of consciousness. Something old has to end so that something new can come to be. In the initiation rights of tribal cultures, this step is often made as a symbolic death where a person leaves behind an old condition to be reborn, healed and initiated. Wolfram von Eschenbach describes this experience in Gawain's adventures in the magic castle, and in his encounter with the Duchess Orgeluse of Logrois.

Searching for the mysterious castle with the imprisoned women, Gawain rode through many countries. He asked everywhere, but nobody knew the way. One day, Gawain rode through a fertile grove where figs, pomegranates, olive trees and grapevines grew. At a spring, he found a beautiful woman, Duchess Orgeluse of Logrois. For her love, many a knight had lost his head and his life. Anfortas, too, had once fallen in love with her. In her service he had broken the laws of the Grail, and been wounded by a poisoned spear.

Gawain was fascinated by her extraordinary beauty. She was 'his luck and the pain of his heart'. She made fun of him, and suggested that he find another love. 'You are many miles from my heart, and if you enter into my service you will get into serious trouble.' For Gawain, her beauty was like a call, and he was determined to follow it. The Duchess warned him again, but realizing his determination she asked him to get a horse from her garden. Gawain was overjoyed. In her garden he found beautiful women and knights who happily sang and danced together. When they saw Gawain, however, their joy turned to despair. A loud wailing began. Gawain rode through the despairing people, and under an olive tree he found the Duchess's horse. It was white on one side and black on the other. The horse was guarded by a wounded knight who, when he saw Gawain, burst into tears. 'Turn around and leave this horse here,' he said, and cursed the Duchess who had sent to many knights to their death. But Gawain took the reins of the horse and led it to his mistress.

'You are a fool to enter my service,' said the Duchess, and when Gawain wanted to help her into the saddle, she rejected him roughly. She mounted her horse and rode off. Gawain followed her. After a while, they found a woman under a tree holding a wounded knight in her lap. She was crying. Gawain, who knew the art of healing, descended from his horse, and with his hands dug a root out of the ground. The Duchess laughed at him and mocked him as he put a bandage on the wounded knight.

Gawain had met this knight before. Many years ago it was he who had violated a virgin in King Arthur's land, and the crown had wanted to hang him. Following

Gawain's plea on his behalf, the knight was pardoned. As a punishment, however, for one month he had to eat with the dogs from a trough. The knight had never forgotten this experience. When Gawain helped him now, he recognised him, and asked him to help his wife onto the horse so she could find help. When Gawain lifted the woman onto the horse, however, the wounded knight jumped onto Gawain's horse and rode off with his wife.

When the proud Orgeluse found her knight tricked out of his horse, she laughed at him. 'First I thought you were a knight, then a doctor, and now you walk on foot like a servant.'

Now a strange person came along on a miserable nag. It was Malcreature, the court jester, whose body was deformed, his hair grey and red like the spikes of a hedgehog. 'Get off your horse, Malcreature, and give it to this knight,' said the Duchess, and unwillingly the dwarf descended from his horse. 'If you wish to accompany me you will have to be content with this horse,' then said the Duchess to Gawain, but when he mounted the nag it almost collapsed and he could barely follow the Duchess.

Orgeluse and Gawain rode through a dense forest. Soon they reached a wide stream where a ferryman was waiting. Gawain saw on the other side of the river a gigantic grey marble castle built into the rock. Through its windows he saw women who, dreamlike, stared into the valley without moving. When he turned to the Duchess, he saw an armed knight galloping straight towards him. The Duchess, however, was already in the middle of the river. 'When will I see you again?' called Gawain, and she answered, 'Only if you win this battle will you see me again. You will see, I did not promise too much, because now you will be in trouble. Defend yourself as well as you can, because this knight is dangerous. With his lance, he will throw you off your battle-horse.'

On the other side of the river was a land where the magician, Klingsor, kept the women prisoners in a castle. At the threshold to this 'other world' Gawain had to fight a battle with the guardian of the threshold. Already with the first blow, his horse sank to its knees and fell. Gawain, however, succeeded in grasping his opponent around the waist, and with force he threw him to the ground. they then continued the fighting with swords. In the end, the knight had to surrender. Only then did Gawain recognize his opponent's horse: it was his own Gringuljete, which he had lost through the trickery of the wounded knight.

The ferryman took Gawain across the river and invited him to spend the night in his house. Gawain accepted with pleasure, and the ferryman's wife prepared a hearty meal. After dinner, Gawain was led to a room full of bulrushes and flowers. He felt comfortable here, and soon fell into a deep sleep. Before dawn, Gawain awoke and walked out into the garden. The women of the castle were still sitting motionless at their windows; they did not sleep. Gawain was surprised. He returned to bed and slept again. When he awoke, he found Bene, the ferryman's daughter, at his bedside. She smiled at him, but when he asked her about the women in the castle she was terrified, and began to cry. She did not want to tell him anything. The ferryman, too, was alarmed at Gawain's questions. 'Oh, do not ask us,' he said, 'because the suffering up there is indescribable.' When Gawain persisted with his questions, the ferryman told him of Klingsor's magic castle: 'You are in a magic land here and the castle up there is the "Schastel Marveile". Four queens and four-hundred women are held captive there by a magician. Many knights have tried to free the women but none of them has left the castle alive. Whoever can survive the trials in the castle, however, will have freed the women and the land from the magician's spell.'

The ferryman asked Gawain to return, but Gawain was determined to ride to the magic castle to free the imprisoned women. To protect Gawain from danger, the ferryman gave him a shield and then led him up to the 'Schastel Marveile'. At the castle, Gawain gave his horse to a merchant who, from a tent of velvet, was selling the most beautiful objects from East and West. Inside the castle Gawain found a great meadow. Through a door that was carved of ivory and ebony, he entered the main hall. The floor of the hall was made of precious stones which shone green, red, indigo and blue. Its light was mirrored mysteriously by the vaulted ceiling. The windows, too, were richly decorated. In the window niches he found couches covered with precious blankets. This is where the ladies whom Gawain had seen during the night might have sat. Now, however, the hall was empty. The whole castle was deserted and lifeless.

From the hall, Gawain reached a second room that was also covered with precious stones. The walls were of marble and in the center he found a large bed, decorated with silver strings and bells. Four dwarfs with grim faces carved in stone carried the bed on their shoulders. They stood on wheels of sparkling rubies. The floor of the hall was so smooth that upon the smallest movement the bed began to roll. When Gawain approached the bed, it seemed to move away. Whenever he took a step, the bed began to move. Again and again the bed rolled away from him and so, when it seemed to become still, Gawain jumped up and landed in its center. The golden bed now began to move furiously. the silver bells were ringing loudly and the whole palace echoed as the bed crashed into the marble walls. Gawain tried to hold on, but soon felt giddy. He became sick. Again and again, the bed rammed the stone walls unceasingly, so Gawain put the shield over his head and surrendered to his destiny. And after a while the roaring ended, and the beautiful bed came to rest in the middle of the room.

This, however, was just the beginning. From five-hundred invisible catapults, stones began to rain down on him. Gawain hid under the ferryman's shield, but when the catapults became silent he was bombarded with arrows from five-hundred invisible crossbows. Then the magic finished as suddenly as it began. Gawain felt the pain of his bruises and wounds.

Suddenly a door opened and a horrid-looking servant entered the room. His clothes were like the skin of a sea-otter, and in his hand he held a heavy club. When Gawain saw the servant, he drew his sword; and when the servant saw Gawain still alive, he hesitated and angrily left the room.

From far away Gawain heard a loud roaring, and when the door opened again a gigantic lion jumped into the room. He was as large as a horse and his roar echoed through the whole castle. With his first jump the lion's claws penetrated Gawain's shield. Gawain, however, fought with all his strength and finally cut off the lion's paws. Again and again the wounded animal jumped at him, and the floor was covered in blood. In the end, however, Gawain succeeded in killing the lion with his sword. He sank exhausted to the floor. It was utterly silent in the castle.

Later, a door opened hesitantly, and when the ladies entered the room they found Gawain on the floor. He was heavily injured; his head was on the lion's belly and it seemed as if he was dead. The women took off his helmet and his armour, and the old queen, Arnive, dressed his wounds with a cream from Cundry, the sorceress of the Grail Castle. When Arnive gave him a sleeping draught, he fell asleep on the spot.

Gawain had mastered the trials in the magic castle. To free the women of Klingsor's enchantment, he had to cross the boundaries of his awareness. On the magic bed, he crashed against the marble walls of his own consciousness. To enter into the realms beyond conscious thought, he had to let go of the limitations of his awareness and surrender to his destiny. In this way, the bed could come to rest in the middle of the room — in Gawain's own centre.

To redeem the spiritual realm of the Grail, Gawain had to free the enchanted forces of the soul in the magic castle. If the spirit is not connected to the soul, it becomes rigid and lifeless. It was Gawain's task to anchor the spirit in the realm of the soul. In his adventures, he had to be touched in all parts of his self. In the language of

Alchemy: he had to integrate all four elements.

His trials in the magic castle were encounters with the forces of the four elements. From the earth came the stones that rained down on Gawain. Within a person, they correspond to the body. From the air, Gawain was hit by arrows — a symbol of the spirit and the breath; Gawain had to deal with these forces. He encountered the element water in the guise of a giant dressed in the skin of an otter — an embodiment of the power of emotion. Finally, in his battle with the lion, Gawain mastered the forces of fire. This was the most dangerous part of his trials. When the battle was over, he lay almost lifeless on the dead lion.

With the trials of the magic castle, Wolfram shows a holistic understanding of personal development. To grow, a person has to develop all parts. In the symbolic language of alchemy, he has to realize the forces of each element within himself.

If, for example, we try to solve key questions of our lives by merely analyzing them, and if we exclude our capacity to feel, our personal development will be limited. At the same time, if we deal exclusively with our feelings and unresolved suffering from childhood, we are limited as well. For a person who is alienated from himself, the release of feelings can be a great healing. It is, however, only a part of the journey. Once the water qualities are redeemed, we can develop our spiritual capacities (which correspond to the element air). To unfold our true potential, we will also need to awaken inspiration (fire) which gives meaning to our lives, and we will need to deal with the reality of the body (earth). Only through the interplay of all four elements can be become whole.

Gawain awoke at the break of dawn. His wounds were hurting badly, but his longing for Orgeluse did not let him sleep any longer. Restless, he wandered through the palace.

In the main hall, he found a spiral staircase which led into a tower. With great effort, he climbed the steps and at the top discovered a large column covered with diamonds, amethysts, topazes, garnets, crystalites and rubies. Never before had Gawain seen such a miracle. The precious stones radiated every color, and it seemed as if in their light he could see the surroundings of the castle. Then the old queen, Arnive, entered the tower, accompanied by Gawain's mother, Sangive, and his sisters, Itonje and Kundrie. The women praised him and he thanked them for their care.

The old queen explained to Gawain the secret of the magic column. Klingsor, the magician, had brought it from a country in the East. It was indestructible and its power radiated day and night. Whatever happened within six miles could be seen in its light. As Gawain listened to the old queen he suddenly discovered in the light of the column Duchess Orgeluse riding with an armed knight. Gawain's longing became unbearable and immediately he wanted to find the Duchess and fight with the knight. The women warned Gawain about the malicious Duchess and the dangerous knight. 'You should never leave this castle,' said the old queen mother, 'or you will bring great injustice to us.'

'It would be a poor reward if I were to become a prisoner myself,' answered Gawain, and prepared himself for the battle. His wounds caused him great pain, but his longing was so intense that he mounted his horse and left the castle.

With the help of the ferryman Gawain crossed the river again, and in battle defeated the strange knight. Duchess Orgeluse had watched this battle from a distance, and when she saw the lion's claws on his shield her eyes became dark. 'You must be very proud of this battle,' she said. 'The women in the castle regard you as a great hero. Go and let them cure you, because what I wish from you, you would never dare.' Gawain was happy to see the Duchess again, and did not care about her mockery. For her love, he was ready to go through all trials and adventures, and when the ladies in the castle saw him riding off with the Duchess, they believed him lost forever.

In silence, Gawain followed the Duchess through a forest. When they reached the edge of a deep ravine with a roaring river, she stopped her horse. Pointing to a tree on the other side of the river, she said, 'If you desire my love, bring me a branch from this tree. It is guarded by a man who has hurt me deeply.'

Gawain saw the tree on the other side of the river. Deep below, he heard the wild roaring of the water. Then he began to gallop and his horse made a giant leap, but the ravine was too wide. Although the horse touched the other side with its front hooves, it fell with Gawain into the depths. The wild water pulled Gawain downstream and his iron armour weighed him down. Gawain fought for his life, and finally he reached a rock and succeeded in saving himself and his horse from the water.

Gawain had crossed another dangerous threshold. Dripping wet, he climbed the bank on the other side. As he broke a branch from the tree, Gawain was met by Gramoflanz, the King of the Forest. Gramoflanz wore a long, green velvet coat. He was riding a mighty horse and on his head he wore a hat with a peacock's feather. On his hand, the king held a sparrow-hawk. 'I have not given this branch to you,' he said haughtily. 'From your shield, I see that you have endured the battles in Klingsor's magic castle. Klingsor and I are friends. The Duchess, in whose service you are, is our enemy. I, too, once tried for her love. I have offered her my kingdom and crown. When she refused, I killed her lover and kidnapped her. I imagine you have come to kill me.'

The King of the Forest was unarmed, but he was still a fearsome knight. His power was so great that he never fought against a single knight. He said that the only knight he would fight alone against would be the famed Sir Gawain, as he believed that Gawain's father had killed his own.

When Gawain revealed his identity, the men prepared for battle. To increase their fame, they decided to invite King Arthur with his entire court and also the women from the magic castle. Upon departure, the King of the

Forest gave Gawain a ring. He had abandoned his love for Orgeluse and was now in love with a lady from the magic castle. Gramoflanz did not know that Itonje was Gawain's sister, and he asked Gawain, as the new master of the castle, to give Itonje the ring.

When Gawain returned across the deep ravine, the Duchess was waiting for him. She was in tears. Gawain watched her in silence, then said, 'I am bringing you the branch as you had wished, but never again should you humiliate a knight in this way. Even your beauty does not give you a right to do so. If you continue to mock me, I will stop trying for your love.'

The pride of the Duchess was now broken. In a stream of tears she told him of her misery. She spoke of Cidegast, her lover, and the many knights that she had sent into battle to avenge his death. Anfortas, too, had tried for her love, and in her service he was injured. The Duchess asked Gawain to forgive her, and together they rode into the redeemed magic castle.

Chapter 15
The Goddess of the Wild

The encounter between Gawain and Gramoflanz resembles a ritual of the Roman Goddess, Diana. James Frazer has described this ritual in *The Golden Bough*: Diana was a Goddess of the Moon and the wild. In her sanctuary was a tree guarded by a strong man. The tree was an expression of her force of life. The wild man was a priest as well as a king, strong and dangerous. When his power diminished he was killed in battle by his successor, who then guarded the tree in his place.

> 'He was at once a priest and murderer; the man for whom he was watching was sooner or later to murder him and hold the priesthood in his stead. For such was the rule of the sanctuary: a candidate for the priesthood could succeed to office only by slaying the incumbent priest in single combat ... Moreover — and this is especially significant — he could fling his challenge only if he had first succeeded in plucking a golden bough from the tree which the priest was guarding.'
>
> (James Frazer, *The Golden Bough*)

Through the ritual killing of the old priest, the force of life was renewed. It could awake in his successor.

Wolfram von Eschenbach also calls Gramoflanz the King of the Forest. Instead of serving the 'Goddess', however, he had turned against her. When Orgeluse had refused his love, he killed her lover and abducted her. Together with the magician, Klingsor, he ruled the country where the women were held captive in a magic castle.

In her battle with the King of the Forest, the power of

the 'Goddess' had frozen. Orgeluse was trapped in her own suffering and unable to redeem herself. In order to become free, she had sent many knights into the dangerous battle with Gramoflanz, but none of them was successful. When Gawain brought her the branch of the tree, however, the spell was broken. She wept. She was redeemed, and the force of life could flow again.

For Gawain the Duchess was a classical Anima figure who led him to the hidden, lunar parts of his soul. In his adventure with Gramoflanz, he redeemed the power of a moon goddess. In the re-enactment of an ancient ritual, he was initiated into the realm of the moon goddess, the feminine side of the soul. The symbolic meaning of this adventure is apparent. It becomes even clearer by looking at the qualities of this moon goddess in greater depth.

Diana — in Greece she was called Artemis — was truly feminine, a virgin, and goddess of sexuality as well. (To be a virgin — Parthenos — did not originally signify sexual abstinence. It meant that a woman did not belong to a man, that she was unmarried. The temple prostitutes themselves were virgins. In giving themselves to men, they united with their goddess.) Artemis/Diana embodied a rejection of the rule of patriarchy. In contrast with many other goddesses, she did not belong to a (male) god. Like Dame Ragnell, she claimed her self-determination. As a Moon Goddess, Diana/Artemis was also a goddess of the earth and nature. She embodies a direct and spiritual relation to nature:

> 'The woods and fields belong to Artemis and her nymphs: each tree, laurel or myrrh, oak or ash, is truly recognized only when we know with which nymphs to associate it; each wild flower, each brook and stream, also evokes a particular sacred presence. Artemis ... bespeaks a loving respect for the unique essence of everything as it lives in its natural state ... her response is animistic, anima-istic. Each creature — each plant, each wood, each river — is to her a Thou, not an It.'
>
> (Christian Downing, *The Goddess*)

Diana of Ephesus (second-century alabaster and bronze, National Museum of Archaeology, Naples, Italy).

As huntress, Artemis/Diana is the protectress of the young and unborn life. She protected the young animals of the wild, and pregnant women prayed to her for the wellbeing of their unborn children. Artemis was also a goddess of fertility, and sometimes she was portrayed as a primal mother with many breasts. The flow of life was sacred to her. She brought rain which enables plants, animals and people to grow. At the same time, however, she could destroy life through storms and floods. Like the moon, she had a bright and a dark side.

Artemis represents the capacity for change. Like the Indian God, Shiva, she was a goddess of death and birth. Her immortality was the eternal rhythm of the waxing and waning moon. As the moon waxes once it has waned, she renews life in a continuous dance of death and birth. In difficult changes and in life transitions, Artemis/Diana was a protecting goddess who led people back into harmony with the natural rhythms of life. These are the inner rhythms of a person as well as the rhythms of nature. It is the rhythms of the heart, the endless inhaling and exhaling of the breath, or the menstrual cycle of women. It is the inner rhythms that all life follows. In nature, it is the cycle of the seasons, the change of day and night, and the growth cycles of plants. Each planet and each living cell is rooted in these rhythms.

Corresponding to the phases of the moon, this goddess was depicted in three different ways: as Artemis/Diana she corresponded to the waxing moon; all growth was sacred to her. As Selene, she embodied the power of the full moon. As Hecate, she was a goddess of the underworld, corresponding to the waning, dark phase of the moon.

When Gawain found Duchess Orgeluse, life had dried up in its flow. The King of the Forest had turned against the Duchess, and in his realm a castrated magician held the women prisoners in a castle. In the world of the Grail, however, a sick king reigned who could neither live nor die. Both realms were mysteriously connected and both (Anfortas as well as Gramoflanz) wore a peacock's feather on their hat. The peacock is a symbol of rebirth and the eternal cycle of life. In the first ten centuries of Christianity, the peacock was a symbol of Christ who lived through death to rise to new life.

Gawain's call was to free life from its stagnation. Led by the mistress of his soul, he lived through an ancient ritual of the Goddess Diana. To free life, Gawain had to live through the cycle of life, death and rebirth within himself. In his initiation, he touched the threshold of death. As in the ancient rights of initiation, he descended into an underworld to re-emerge again with the power of new life.

With Gawain's adventures Wolfram illustrates the importance of the threshold of death in the unfolding of all life. Every person's inner development unfolds through many deaths and new births. Death is an essential experience in our lives, a necessary part in the cycle of life. It is everywhere. In every moment, we die and are born again. Death is the transition from one moment to the next, a threshold between worlds. It is the final surrender of the old so that the new can come to be.

To unite with the flow of life, the Navajo Indians used to burn their entire belongings every six years. This, too, was a death, a letting go to become free for new life.

Nowadays, it is difficult to accept the experience of death and often we repress an awareness of it. In order not to see it, we banish it — like the experience of birth — into clinics and hospitals. With medical technology, we set out to fight it.

Death makes us afraid. It seems to take from us everything that we have built up with great effort. Often we meet it with a bulwark of external defences. We have life insurance and pensions, and to protect ourselves against all eventualities we hang on to our possessions. By banishing death from our awareness, however — and with it the experience of letting go — we distance ourselves from the natural rhythms that all life follows. We hold on and begin to live arhythmically. To make up for our unlived life, we then fall back on memories and glorified hopes for the future.

Physical death might then be the painful moment when we have to let go of all comforting hopes and memories to return to our true rhythm. In death we can only be totally ourselves. Then we might become aware how far we have separated ourselves from the flow of life. It might be the moment when our illusions are shattered. If we have not really lived, we might then suffer from unlived and missed opportunities.

If we live in harmony with the inner rhythms, death is a constant companion. It is the threshold to new experiences and new dimensions. Physical death at the end of life is then just another experience, requiring to be fully lived, a threshold that opens onto another world.

I remember the death of my grandfather: he had been a man with a strong life-force. As a painter, he was fascinated by the colors of life. In his last years — by then he was in his nineties — he had learnt to surrender to the flow of life, and in closeness to death, something seemed to open inside him. Like a wise child, he regarded life as one great miracle. At that time he believed that he was no longer creating art, but he told of the forces within him that wanted to be realized. The talents he had developed in ninety-four years were now in the service of these forces. The outcome of this he called 'ways of being human'. They were images of moments in faces and masks; moments of life. In spite of increasing blindness, these pictures emerged with great force from inside him. On the day of his death, we had a long conversation. Utterly relaxed, he told me how incredibly soothing it was now to let go. In this letting go, life seemed to realize itself again in its totality. He was at ease and fully alive. Like a plant, he seemed to bloom once more. During the night, he left us. His last words were, 'I bless you in gratefulness and love'.

In these moments, I have learned something about the essence of death. I have felt my own pain and felt how hard it was to let go of a loved one. At the same time, however, I have come to know death as a threshold, a final release which opens a new dimension. Alan Watts wrote:

> 'Nothing is more creative than death, since it is the whole secret of life ... Death is the epitome of the truth that in each moment we are thrust into the unknown. Here all clinging to security is compelled to cease, and wherever the past is dropped away and safety abandoned, life is renewed ... When a man knows this he lives for the first time in his life.'
>
> (Alan Watts, *The Wisdom of Insecurity*)

The conscious experience of death is an initiation into the mystery of life. It is a moment where infinity touches finity.

The cycle of life can be experienced in our breath, in the constant flow of inhalation and exhalation. In a guided exercise you can experience this cycle within yourself. The words for this exercise should be read slowly, and in rhythm with the natural flow of your breathing:

Close your eyes, and relax. Let your breath flow deeply. Let go all thoughts and expectations and begin to concentrate on the flow of your breathing.

With every inhalation you take in new life. You nourish every cell in your body with fresh oxygen. With every exhalation you let go of everything your body no longer needs.

Through your breath you are connected with all life. The air that you exhale is nourishment to plants and trees. With every inhalation you take in the oxygen they produce.

The quality of the inhalation is quite different from the quality of the exhalation. Let your breath flow freely and feel the unique quality of your breathing.

Focus your awareness now on the moment where the inhalation becomes exhalation. It is a moment of letting go, the autumn when the leaves fall from the trees.

Now, focus your awareness on the end of your exhal-

ing — a moment of silence, in which a new inhalation comes to be. It is a moment of creation. It is spring-time, when the force of life flows into every cell. Every inhalation is a new birth; every exhalation a final letting go. This rhythm has been with you all of your life. It began with your first breath, and it will end with the last one.

In your imagination you can now travel into the future. Let yourself imagine that you approach the moment of your last breath. You can still feel the rhythm of your breathing, that wonderful exchange. With the flow of your breath you begin to imagine your own death. Maybe you will see images of the place where you will die. Are you alone here, or surrounded by people? Are you close to the people you are with? What do you experience as you approach your own death?

Once again, focus your awareness on the flow of your breathing, the rhythm of life that was with you throughout your life — and then, there is a last inhalation. Once more let the force of life enter your body — and then comes a last, a final, letting go.

With this last breath you enter into another realm. It is the timeless space that lies between exhaling and inhaling. Let yourself explore this space in your imagination and feelings. At the threshold of death, your entire life begins to pass in front of you — you see the moment of your own birth — you see the child that you one were, and the many experiences that you lived through in the course of your life — you see the places and landscapes in which you lived — you see people who were close to you, and the many decisions that you made in the course of your life — you see key experiences, and the pain that you have suffered. As in a film, you see your entire life from the moment of your birth to the moment of death.

From a distance, you can now see your own funeral. You can see the grave into which you will be laid, and the people that are gathered here. Maybe you can hear *what these people are saying.*

Your entire life is spread out in front of you now. What was this life like? What was essential in your life? And how did you live the experiences that were essential to you? Possibly you will also discover experiences that remained unfulfilled and unlived. Did you miss essential things in your life? If you could enter this life one more time, what would you do differently?

You are now in a realm beyond space and time. It is the endless moment between exhalation and a new breath. It is the moment of creation, from which life can unfold once again. From here you can now enter once again into your own life. What remained incomplete can now be lived completely.

Exhale once again, and hold your breath for a moment ... with your next inhalation you are stepping back into your life again. This is like a first breath, in which the flow of life awakens and touches every cell of your body. From here your life can unfold once again and you can live all the things that have remained incomplete. Take a deep breath. Feel the flow of your breathing and the power that awakens in yourself.

Slowly, and with the rhythm of your breathing, you can then return with your awareness into the present moment. Let yourself stretch, and when you are ready, open your eyes.

The awareness of death leads to new life. If we do not banish death from our awareness, he is a companion who reminds us not to postpone important matters. With death on our side, we can experience the flow of life. We can learn to live life in every moment. Every moment could be a last one. Every encounter with a person could be the last opportunity to speak and realize essential truths.

How would our lives change if we knew that we have only a few more days to live? Maybe we would begin to fully realize the presence of a partner. Maybe we would once again truly meet, touch, laugh or just be together.

Many things that usually seem extraordinarily important would lose their importance. We would become aware of essentials. Maybe we would take the time to see the colors of nature, or to play with a child that we love. Possibly we would also want to speak with a person with whom we are in discord. Maybe we would become able to forgive each other and start anew. To become clear with another person, it might be necessary to speak about unresolved issues. Once we accept death as a reality, we stop holding on to missed opportunities and hopes about the future. Only then do we become one with the flow of life that happens in every moment.

You can explore this experience for yourself in the following exercise. You will need a large sheet or paper and crayons.

Draw a simple image or symbol of yourself in the centre of the paper. Around it you can then draw images or symbols of people who are important in your life. the shapes and colors will be different for each person. Some will be closer to you than others. You can also include people who are already dead, but continue to be important in your life. This picture is a representation of yourself and the relations that are important in your life.

Imagine now that you have only three more days to live, only three more days to realize all the things that are important to you. Whatever you do not do now will remain undone. As your time is limited, you will concentrate on the essential.

What will you be doing in these three days? On your paper you see the people and relations who are important to you, and maybe you want to be in contact with these people again and say a goodbye. This might also be the moment to say the things which have remained unsaid. It is an opportunity to deal with the unresolved issues in your life, and to complete unfinished business. It is an opportunity to resolve the unresolved and to bring what was stagnated back into process. Here is a possibility of freeing yourself from the burden of the past and rediscovering the flow of life.

Take a moment to explore your picture, and then begin to speak to each person in your drawing. You can also write a letter to the people who are important in your life. If you are with a partner you might want to sit back to back. Your partner can then listen to you as you begin to speak to the people in your drawing. (He or she will not answer you, however.)

Through this process you can enter into contact with the people who are important in your life. As you transform the burden of unresolved issues and feelings into a process, life can flow again.

Parzival's search for the Grail is also an attempt to become clear with the 'unfinished business' of his life. He had failed to ask the crucial question of the heart. To return to the Grail Castle he had to free what he had failed to live before. This inner journey is described in the adventures of Gawain. At the threshold of death, Gawain was able to free life again from stagnation.

Chapter 16
Healing

When Gawain and Orgeluse reached the magic castle, they were received with joy and great celebration. The knights and ladies who had been separated for so long, were dancing and laughing together. Later in the evening, Gawain gave his sister, Itonje, the ring of Gramoflanz. She, too, was secretly in love with the King of the Forest, and when he put the ring into her hands her face became as pink as her lips. 'In thought, I have already granted him all his wishes,' she said, 'he would have known long ago if we hadn't been imprisoned here.'

When Gawain's eyes fell upon the Duchess, it seemed to him as if he had been already too long in the hall. He retired with Orgeluse into a beautiful room. In Wolfram's words, he found here the right remedy for healing himself of all evil.

Meantime, King Arthur had set off with many knights and ladies to witness the battle in Joflanze. When Gawain saw the knights he was overjoyed, and with a beautiful army from the 'Schastel Marveile' he greeted the king. It was many years since he had left the Round Table, and when he embraced the king and the queen, knights and ladies were cheering. With tears in his eyes King Arthur embraced his mother, the old Queen Arnive, and greeted Gawain's mother, the Queen of Norway, with her daughters Itonje and Kundrie. It was a big celebration.

During the night, Gawain could not find rest. Again and again he thought about the next day's battle, and he was concerned that there was no sign yet of Gramoflanz.

At the hour of dawn, Gawain put on his armour. His wounds had not yet healed and his scars caused him great pain. Quietly he took his horse from the stable, and in the first light of day he left the camp.

In the mist of the morning, Gawain saw the outline of a knight. His armour was red like ruby, but his shield was battered and beaten. When Gawain discovered a branch jutting from the knight's helmet, he believed him to be the King of the Forest and prepared himself for battle. The other knight had noticed him too, and with their lances at the ready they galloped towards each other. It was an arduous battle as both knights were accustomed to victory. Again and again they clashed. Gawain received many blows and bled from many wounds.

When Gawain's strength seemed to be dwindling, squires appeared on the field. They had heard the sounds of lances and swords, and when they found Gawain in distress they called out his name. When the strange knight heard Gawain's name, he threw away his sword. It was Parzival. In tears, he lamented having fought against a friend, and Gawain answered: 'Two hearts that are but one have shown their strength in fierce enmity. Your hand has overcome us both. Now regret it for our sakes. If your heart be true, you have subdued yourself.'

With this battle, Wolfram shows again that Parzival and Gawain are really one. Both had to fulfil a task, each in his own way. Now that they had come together again, they embraced with all their heart.

Gawain led Parzival back to the Round Table and again a celebration began. When later the King of the Forest reached the scene, he was told of Gawain's battle with Parzival. As Gawain had been weakened by his wounds, they decided to postpone the battle until the next day, but then another confusion occurred: Gramoflanz fought against Parzival instead of Gawain, and when the mistake was discovered they decided to delay their battle once again.

In the meantime, Itonje had learned from the ferryman's daughter that Gawain was the opponent of her lover. As she did not want to lose either lover or brother, she asked Arthur to reconcile the knights. Even Orgeluse was ready to forgive the King of the Forest. And so, there were many weddings that day: Gawain married Orgeluse, and his sister Itonje married the King of the Forest. They danced all night, and knights and ladies enjoyed themselves by candlelight.

Parzival, however, felt like a stranger in their company. He followed the dancers with sad eyes and the music stirred his heart. He remembered the day he left the Round Table and the many years of wandering. He felt his loneliness and he longed for Condwiramurs. As if in a dream, he left the celebration of the Round Table. He saddled his horse and with the first light of the morning, left the camp.

In a forest, Parzival met a beautiful knight. He was covered in precious stones and his armour was forged by salamanders in the bowels of the earth. On his helmet he wore the picture of a snake. This was an 'Ecidemon' (an animal that brings death to all poisonous snakes). From his heart, however, the stranger radiated a feeling of happiness that only love can give. This knight came from the East. He was accompanied by fifty armies camped close by. To explore the area, he had left his camp, and when he met Parzival he saw the opportunity for an adventure. His eyes shone, and at the next moment, the lances of the two knights crashed against their shields. Both knights, however, remained firmly mounted and a bitter battle began. Wolfram von Eschenbach laments this battle in many a verse.

Each of the knights carried the heart of the other in his chest. They were close even if they were strangers ... both men were of the same flesh and blood yet brought distress to one another. The strange knight was Parzival's brother, Feirefis. Without recognizing each other, the two brothers clashed. They fought a hard battle — 'If one can speak of two knights. In essence they were one and inseparably connected.'

The knight from the East fought in the service of his

lover, Queen Secundille. Her image in his heart gave him strength. Parzival, who fought in the name of God, weakened under the blows of his opponent. He became more and more distressed, but then he too remembered the power of love: he remembered Condwiramurs. As he was about to deal a heavy blow, however, his sword broke on the helmet of his opponent. It was a sword that he had once taken from the Red Knight. Now he was unarmed.

As the stranger did not want to fight against a knight without arms, he offered peace. In silence the two brothers sat down together. The strange knight had never fought a battle as hard as this one, and he asked for the name of his opponent. Parzival, however, felt in his honor injured, and stared in silence at the armour of the stranger. 'Then I will tell you my name first,' said the stranger. 'I am Feirefis of Anjou. I am king of many countries in the East.'

Parzival did not believe him. He himself was the Lord of Anjou. He remembered, however, that he had been told of a brother who lived as a knight in the East. This was the son of Gahmuret and the black queen, Belakane. He had been told that the knight was chequered black and white, like a magpie. Parzival asked the stranger to show his face, and promised not to fight until his helmet was secured again. But the stranger knight answered:

> 'I am not afraid of attack by you. Even if I were totally unarmed, you would lose because I have a sword while yours in broken. Before you could try your luck in wrestling, my sword would penetrate your armour and your chest. If the battle should start again, neither of us should have an advantage.'

And Feirefis then took his sword and threw it into a thicket. When he took off his helmet, the brothers recognised each other. They embraced and together rode to King Arthur's camp.

Parzival's departure had hurt the king deeply, and he had hoped that Parzival would return. Through Klingsor's magic column they had watched the battle of the brothers, and when they reached the camp Feirefis was admitted into the Order of the Round Table. Knights and ladies admired his chequered skin and precious clothes.

The next day was the celebration of Pentecost. The Round Table was surrounded by many people who were fed delicious food and drink. It was a wonderfully happy day, and when Feirefis saw the many women, his heart was full of joy. Then, as once before, a woman rode into the circle of knights and ladies. Her velvet coat was as black as the skin of her horse. She wore a white hat with a veil over her face, and on her dress was embroidered a golden dove, the symbol of the Grail. They saw her coming from afar: at a canter she crossed the field, and rode into the happy circle of knights. This time she greeted the King and Queen and then fell to her knees in front of Parzival. She asked him to bury his anger and to forgive her.

When she rose, she took the veil from her head and threw it into the circle. Now she was recognised: it was once again Cundry, the sorceress. Her face was still covered with hair, her eyes yellow like topaz, her teeth were long and her mouth deformed and blue like a violet. 'Rejoice,' she said to Parzival, 'because a writing on the Grail said that you are now called to redeem the king and become the new King of the Grail. Condwiramurs and your son, Loherangrin, shall accompany you.' It was only then that Parzival learnt that the Queen had born him two sons, Kardeis and Loherangrin. His suffering was over. He was called to the Grail. Cundry said:

> 'All sadness is now over. All your suffering will disappear, but beware of excess. Your youth was accompanied by sorrow, but the joy that awaits you now will disperse it. You have borne the suffering until you found joy and peace of the soul. Now you are redeemed.'

Cundry told Parzival now in Arabic the names of the planets:

> 'Take note, Parzival: the loftiest planet Zval [Saturn] and swift Almustri [Jupiter], Almaret [Mars] and bright Samsi [the Sun] point to good fortune for you. The fifth

> planet is called Alligafir [Venus], and the sixth, Alkiter [Mercury], while the nearest to us is Alkamer [the Moon] ... Everything that the planets embrace within their orbits, whatever they shed their light on, marks the scope of what there is for you to attain and achieve. Your sorrow is destined to pass away ...'

Parzival wanted to return immediately to the Grail Castle and his departure was prepared for at once. Cundry asked him to bring Condwiramurs and Loherangrin and one other person with him to the Grail. 'One man may go as your companion. Choose him. for guidance look to me. Because of the vital help you will bring, do not delay.' Parzival asked his brother, Feirefis, to accompany him, and on the same day they started off on their journey.

Through the planets, Cundry showed the knights aspects of a wholeness in which all essential forces are contained. On his journey, Parzival had moved through the spheres of all the planets. Through his adventures, he had allowed the uninvited gods into his life; he had redeemed the forces of his being. Now he would be able to redeem the Grail.

In astrology, the planets embody the forces of the universe which work in each person in specific constellations. On a journey to wholeness, a person needs to discover the qualities of all the planets within themselves:

The Sun is the symbol of consciousness. It embodies the will and the creative forces of a person. In Jung's *Analytical Psychology* it corresponds to an inner masculine principle.

The Moon is the symbol of the feminine. It embodies the world of feelings and emotions. It is an access to the depth of the soul.

Mercury is the planet of exchange and communication. In Greek mythology, it was ascribed to Hermes, the messenger of the gods. He embodies the capacity to relate. Within the human body, Mercury corresponds to the nervous system.

Venus is the planet home of the goddess Aphrodite. She embodies the power of love, beauty and harmony.

Mars is a planet of will and self-determination. He embodies the joy of activity. In mythology, the war god Ares is likened to Mars. Like Sun and Moon, Mars and Venus are a classical couple. Both pairs embody the polarity of Yin and Yang which forms the basis of all life processes.

Jupiter embodies the power of higher religion and the search for meaning. Zeus is the god of this planet.

Saturn, planet of death and order, embodies the capacity to learn and to bring experiences fully into consciousness. Saturn is the guardian of the threshold between the seven 'inner' planets and the 'outer' planets.

Uranus, Neptune and *Pluto* had not been discovered in the Middle Ages. In the totality of all planets, however, they play an important role:

Uranus embodies the power to break stagnated structures in order to enlarge all existing order. It is a principle of high tension, urging sudden discharge, and also embodies the power of intuition.

Neptune is a planet of longing. It corresponds to the capacity to transcend limitations to become one with the whole. Neptune is the god of the oceans, and Dionysos, too, is ascribed to this planet. Neptune embodies mystic ecstasy but also fears and chaos.

Pluto, finally, is a planet of deep changes. It embodies a deep feminine principle which realizes itself through many deaths and new births.

When Cundry expresses oneness with the image of the planets, she shows Parzival his inter-relatedness with the entire universe. She does not separate him from the world around him. Like Artemis/Diana, she affirms a person's unity with all life.

When Parzival visited the Grail Castle for the first time, he was separated from the suffering of his uncle. It did not matter to him. In his consciousness, he was separated from his environment as well as from himself. Through the conscious experience of his own suffering, he eventually became one with himself and the people around him.

From separation, Parzival had stepped into unity. To return to the Grail Castle he had to bring along his brother. As well as Condwiramurs and Loherangrin, Feirefis was to accompany him to the Grail. In a way they were parts of his own self. He was man, woman and child at the same time. He was in harmony with the many parts of his being.

Cundry led Parzival and Feirefis into the world of the Grail. The king's suffering was still undiminished and Anfortas was in unbearable pain. To lessen the bad smell from his wound, the Grail knights piled spices and roots around his bed. The king wanted to die. For days at a time, he kept his eyes closed, but the power of the Grail kept him alive. When Parzival reached the Grail Castle, the king's pain was particularly acute. Mars and Jupiter had reached their zenith and Anfortas was suffering badly:

> 'Knights and maidens both heard his cries and saw the doleful glances he gave them. His wound was beyond all cure: there was nothing they could do for him. Nevertheless, the story says real help was now on its way to him.'

When the brothers entered the world of the Grail, they were met by a group of Grail knights on their horses. Feirefis was immediately ready for battle. When the knights recognised Cundry, however, they took off their helmets. Overjoyed and with tears in their eyes, they accompanied the riders to Munsalvasche. Parzival and Feirefis were greeted on the steps leading to the palace. They were led inside the castle and given clothes cut from the same cloth.

When Parzival entered his sick uncle's room, the king recognised him. In agony, he asked him to cover the Grail for a week so that he could die. Parzival was deeply touched. In tears, he fell to the ground and prayed for the healing of the king. Then he looked at Anfortas and asked the redeeming question, 'What ails thee?'.

Through this heartfelt question the king's suffering was redeemed. His face began to radiate miraculous beauty — Parzival had freed his life from its stagnation.

In the meantime, Condwiramurs had left Pelrapeire with her sons. Parzival rode off to meet her with a group of Grail knights, and on his way he came again to the house of the hermit, Trevrizent. When the old man heard of the healing of his brother, he was overjoyed and praised God for His grace. Parzival's return to the Grail was for him a miracle which transcended the limits of his beliefs. Again Parzival thanked the old man for the advice and encouragement he had given him before. Then he continued his journey.

He rode all night. At dawn he came to the place where he had once found the blood in the snow. It was here that he found Condwiramur's camp. The Queen was still asleep when Parzival entered the tent. At her side, he found the two boys. Parzival watched the sleeping children with joy — it was five years since he had left Pelrapeire. When Condwiramurs awoke, she saw her beloved. As she was wearing only a shirt, she drew a blanket around herself and embraced Parzival with both arms. Duke Kyot let the boys be carried away and asked the women to leave the lovers alone. From outside, he closed the tent.

When the sun was already high in the sky, they celebrated a Mass, and Parzival's son, Kardeis, was crowned King of Valois and Kanvoleis. The new king was honored by all the knights, and from his two small hands the Dukes received their lands for tenure. Condwiramurs said goodbye to Kardeis and her people. The Grail knights took her into their midst and with Parzival and Loherangrin, they rode to Munsalvasche.

It was a long journey. After many hours, the riders came to a solitary hut. It was the home of Sigune. When Parzival opened the door, he found the woman by the coffin of her lover, her hands still clasped in prayer, but her body now lifeless. Deep in prayer, she had died by her lover's coffin. In death, they were united. Parzival had the coffin opened and looked at the beautiful face of the embalmed knight. He lay Sigune beside him, and then closed the coffin. In silence, they continued their journey.

When they reached the Grail Castle, it was filled with light. In welcome, so many candles were lit that it seemed as if the whole forest was in flames. Parzival was now the new King of Munsalvasche. In his presence, the Grail procession was once again enacted. As at his first visit, there were fires of Aloe wood burning. They brought in tables and golden cups. Again, four-and-twenty women in festive gowns entered the hall. In their midst, Repanse de Schoye carried the Grail through the hall. The power of the Grail shone brightly. It gave nourishment to all the people. The bleeding lance, however, was missing from the procession; the people were happy and elated.

Feirefis could not understand how the golden cups were filled with food and drink. He was unable to see the Grail, and his eyes were locked on the woman who carried the Grail in her hands; her beauty filled him with longing. Feirefis did not touch the food, and when Anfortas saw the joy of his guest diminishing, he said:

> 'I am sorry, sir, if my sister is the cause of your suffering pangs such as no man endured for her before. No knight has ridden out to serve her, so none has ever had reward of her. She has been at my side in great sorrow, and her looks have suffered somewhat from her having had so little pleasure ...'

To gain her love, Feirefis decided to be baptized. And after baptism in the waters of the Grail, he, too, was able to see the Grail. Repanse de Schoye was, herself in love with the black and white knight, and after a life of chastity she married Feirefis.

Like Gawain, Feirefis embodied another part of Parzival's being. In Gawain, Parzival met the forces of his soul; in Feirefis, he touched the physical level. The armour of his brother was covered with precious stones and the world of minerals relates in a person to the bodily level. This encounter with the physical level was a new challenge to Parzival. He was already familiar with the realm of the spirit and the soul. The battle with his brother, however, was the hardest battle he had ever fought. In his link with Feirefis, Parzival united the spiritual/emotional with the physical level of his being.

Feirefis is also a representative of the earthly world. As ruler of many countries of the East, he accompanies Parzival to the Grail. While Parzival and Condwiramurs will remain at the Grail Castle, Feirefis will return to the earthly world. It is he who will bring the power of the Grail back into the community. Only with his return is the 'Hero's Journey' complete.

Wolfram von Eschenbach shows that the spiritual and the emotional require a link with the world. Parzival's initiation does not lead to a separation from the world. On the contrary, in his search for the Grail, Parzival enters into an existential relationship with the world. He lives through its suffering and its crises. Through his adventures, he becomes able to ask the question of the Grail.

At the end of the legend, the life-force is carried back into the world. Anfortas is healed. Repanse de Schoye leaves her angel-like role as the Grail carrier, and enters a new life. With Feirefis, she sets out into the world. It was a grand farewell. At the same time, it was a new beginning. In India, Repanse gave birth to a son who, as Prestor John, was to teach a mystic Christianity in the East. Parzival was the new king in Munsalvasche. Together with Condwiramurs, he led a rich life in the service of the Grail. The land that had once turned to desert, began to blossom again.

Chapter 17
Myths and Rituals

> 'When the Baal Shem had a difficult task before him, he would go to a certain place in the woods, light a fire and meditate in prayer — and what he had set out to perform was done. When a generation later the "Maggid" of Meseritz was faced with the same task he would go to the same place in the woods and say: "We can no longer light the fire, but we can still speak the prayers" — and what he wanted done became reality. Again, a generation later Rabbi Moshe Leib of Sassov had to perform this task. And he too went into the woods and said: "We can no longer light the fire nor do we know the secret meditations belonging to the prayer, but we do know the place in the woods to which it all belongs — and that must be sufficient." And sufficient it was. But when another generation had passed and Rabbi Israel of Rishin was called upon to perform the task, he sat down on his golden chair in his castle and said: "We cannot light the fire, we cannot speak the prayers, we do not know the place, but we can tell the story of how it was done." And the story which he told had the same effect as the actions of the other three.'
>
> (Gerschom Scholem, *Major Trends in Jewish Mysticism)*

Myths and fairy tales are a bridge to the rituals of long-forgotten times. In the course of history and changes in culture, these rituals were often no longer practised. If the issues they addressed were essential, though, these rituals did not die out but were passed on to succeeding generations in the form of stories or songs. If we open ourselves to the images of these stories, we can rediscover the power of the old rituals and thus find creative and lively ways to reunite with hidden parts of ourselves.

Through the images of myths and legends, and by

entering into a creative process with these images, we can experience the still uninvited gods within ourselves. To invite these gods consciously into our lives, however, and to integrate them, is often a much more difficult task. The redeeming of qualities in our own lives often requires a conscious step. In myths, this is described as the task of the hero. In our own lives we are the heroes, and we have to take these steps ourselves.

In earlier times, and in tribal societies, such conscious steps to integrate a new quality were often made in a ritual context and with the support of the tribe. A ritual was a special framework through which a person could reach beyond his own limitations to meet, in a symbolic drama, the challenges of the world and the still undiscovered powers in his own being. Through rituals, people experienced the reality of these forces and were able to integrate them without being overwhelmed.

In their ceremonies, people united with the forces of nature. In rituals, they trapped symbolic animals which were necessary for their food. In dance, they personified the gods who worked in nature as well as in people. They celebrated the changes of season and lived through important events and stages in a person's development. Through rituals, people also became familiar with the threshold of death. In their ceremonies they could fully realize that, in the cycle of life, each death is followed by regeneration. When people were later faced with the challenges of life, they could recall the experiences they had already danced, sung and lived. They had already faced their fears — now they were ready.

Today, too, a ritual framework can be of great help when consciously going through the steps of an inner development. The old rituals, however, have become strange to us. Often they have become set in patterns that have no meaning for us. In earlier times, many rituals served collective necessities. They helped people to shape their individual lives to the needs of a community.

In a time when life is full of contradictions, when the social and economic order endangers and destroys nature, the rituals which integrate a person into existing modes of thinking have become questionable. In the search for a ritual framework that allows us to step beyond the limitations of existing ways of thinking, we are thus particularly attracted by the old rites of initiation and shamanistic rituals which are still practised in many tribal societies. Through these rituals, a person is led into realms that are beyond the order and limitations of his culture. On a personal journey, he can thus meet the forces of life and unite with the sacred. Enriched, a person can then carry new impulses into society and renew communal life.

The following account of an Eskimo Shaman is a good example of such an initiation: As a child, Igjagarjuk continually had strange dreams that he could not understand. Unknown beings came and spoke to him. As his parents could not understand these dreams either, they sent for an old Shaman. He put the boy on a sledge and, on an ice-cold night, brought him into the Arctic desert. There he built him an igloo that was just high enough to sit in with crossed legs. Igjagarjuk was not allowed to put his foot on the ground. The old man carried him into the hut and sat him on a strip of fur. He asked him to respond to the great spirit who would appear. He gave him neither food nor drink and left him alone in the desert.

After five days, the old man returned and brought him some water. After fifteen days, he brought him some dried meat and some drink, but that was all. 'Sometimes I died a little,' said Igjagarjuk later. During this time, however, he thought endlessly about the Great Spirit. At the end of his search there appeared the image of a woman who seemed to fly back and forth above him. He never saw this woman again; she became, however, his helping spirit and a power through which he was able to heal from then on.

As in the shamanistic rites of initiation, the search for new rituals focuses on renewal through an inner experience. Myths and legends can be a bridge to such experiences in the depths of the soul.

In the seminars that I lead in many parts of the world, participants sometimes explore a story that means something to them. The choice of story is intuitive and spontaneous. Sometimes a person only remembers an image or the atmosphere of a legend. Possibly he might feel, though, that this story touches something in him, that in its images he can discover something of himself.

By dramatizing this story through guided images and in dance, its contents become personal. It becomes a gateway to personal experience. In guided experiences such as I have described in this book, through dance and elements of Psychodrama, and through Fritz Perls' Gestalt Therapy, we can go on to explore what these images touch in us. This process can lead a person to experiences in his own life. Touched by mythical images, experiences from childhood might be awakened and also longings directly connected with our own being.

By experiencing these images and feelings within a mythical context, the outline of our own journey becomes apparent. To give this journey our own conscious direction, we can then create rituals in which we invite the yet uninvited gods into our lives.

A ritual is a symbolic drama. It is a conscious act which requires a playful, but also a thoughtful, inner attitude. Like the rites of initiation in tribal cultures, a ritual requires a special framework which can be created in many ways. For the American Indians, this is a sacred space. In it, people's images and experiences can be unfolded in a powerful and effective way. With the support of a group, a person can thus open to the hidden forces within himself.

The encounter with Cundry, described earlier, is an example of such a ritual. Within the protective group framework, each participant encountered an embodiment of his own shadow. By entering into an active relationship with our shadow — rather than just examining this concept theoretically — it is possible to integrate some parts of it. Active integration does far more than merely free us from the fear and horror that a shadow aspect can cause in us. It is more than the subjection of the shadow by the conscious self. If a person invites such aspects into his own life, he can actually unite with the diverse forces of his own being.

Rituals can be celebrations. Sometimes they are a direct encounter with the forces and rhythms in nature. They offer the possibility of finding a new vision, and anchoring it in our own experiences. As personal rituals, they are related to the rites of passage in many tribal cultures.

In this way, one woman dramatized in a seminar the change from girl to woman. As a girl, she had never fully experienced this threshold. She was still mourning the loss of her childhood. As she had never fully let her childhood go, she was unable to accept her womanhood. In a symbolic drama, she lived through her child world. There were mysterious places and princesses, girlfriends, dolls, animals, parents and relatives. Following her wish, each member of the group embodied an element from her childhood. With the rhythm of drums and rattles, she encountered these elements in a symbolic dance at the threshold to adulthood. In this way, she could bid farewell to experiences she had previously clung to, and make a conscious decision about the qualities of her child's world which would have a place in her life as an adult.

In another group, a woman who was just about to retire created a ritual to prepare herself for the transition into a new phase of her life. The separation from her professional life caused great anxiety. Through a ritual, she experienced and celebrated in a playful, but very serious way, the forthcoming change. Through a conscious letting go, she prepared for a new beginning.

It is an essential element of these rituals that we develop them ourselves. Their form and content is not given. As in the mysteries of antiquity and in the rites of initiation of tribal society, preparation is an essential part of any ritual. To develop a personal ritual, we have to explore the nature and direction of our own journey. We have to ask questions about the issues and experiences that we need for our own growth and healing. In a ritual, we can give these issues their own shape and take a conscious step on our journey.

A group can support a person in this process. It provides security and creates a structure for an extraordinary experience. At the same time, it offers the opportunity to anchor a personal development in a specific situation. In the shared preparation of a ritual, we can awaken the capacity to deal creatively with our visions and the process of personal growth.

Sometimes a ritual is a very simple action. If this simple action has a special meaning within a ritual context, however, it can be developed very effectively. In a group of people of very different ages, an older person at the end of his life developed a ritual to meet the experience of his own death.

At first, he celebrated life in a symbolic dance with the group. In a procession, he was then carried to a hillside. Sitting on a chair, he was covered with a cloth. The other members of the group, all much younger than he was, stood at first behind him, then passed him slowly and in silence. He was left behind alone. He had found his own end, but life continued.

Some time later, he returned to the circle of the group. The depth of his experience was reflected in his face. In drama, he had lived through a process that touched everyone deeply. Through a simple action, he had faced an essential experience in his life. At the same time, his ritual had enriched the community.

Creative work with rituals is a living access to experiences on our own journey. A ritual is a means by which we can open to the great questions and mysteries of life in order to find new answers and solutions from the depth of the soul. The rituals and guided journeys that emerge from our work with myths and fairy tales are often related to 'The Hero's Journey'. Like the old rites of initiation, they lead us across a threshold to another realm. Here we can meet the forces and issues that we require to become whole. Consciously, we can live through experiences that we have not yet faced. We can become whole. Enriched and enriching, we can then return into the community.

When the cycles of past experiences are completed, we are again in the flow of life, ready for new experiences.

Chapter 18
Healing The Wasteland

As we come to the end of this century our sense of story is changing dramatically. As people in all parts of the world are becoming aware and concerned about the destruction of forests, the rapid extinction of species, the nuclear threat and the degradation of soil, they are also becoming aware of the story of our planet. Our individual life journeys are a part of the tapestry of this story that we all share. In exploring people's individual journeys it is growing clear that global environmental issues are becoming an integral part of our sense of biography. As more and more people awaken to the larger picture, we come to see our individual life journeys as part of that tapestry. Images from this larger story are entering our dreams, they influence our choices for the future. Increasingly, we begin to see how the ways we live our lives contribute to this story; and how our actions can influence its direction.

It is at a crucial point within this larger story that our consciousness enters the stage. In the destruction of our life-support system we are faced, again, with our own shadow. But this time it is not just the individual shadow, but a cultural shadow, the shadow of our civilization.

We are now faced with all the things that we have consistently excluded from our awareness as we pursued the dream of unlimited technological expansion. We are facing our shadow in mountains of waste and in the form of poisons that are buried in the ground. We thought we would not have to deal with them any more. But they have been seeping into the ground water and are now returning as uninvited gods into our foodchain and the foodchain of countless other species. Cundry is riding again. We meet her on the nuclear waste sites, we see her in the oil spills in the oceans, and the toxic wastes in the air, the waters and the soil.

As we come face to face with the shadow of this century's technological progress we begin to realize that we have come to the end of an outmoded chapter of life on Earth. We begin to see that in order to continue life, we must not only confront and integrate our individual shadows, but also the shadow aspects of our larger story. To survive we need to find a new way of being.

Through the media we are bombarded with news of the myriad areas of our lives where toxicity has been mounting, and now demands our attention. The destruction of the world's rainforests, the extinction of countless species, nuclear accidents, industrial and chemical discharges into the oceans and streams, the greenhouse effect and the depletion of the ozone layer ... the list goes on and on. It is a frightening image of our cultural shadow.

It is a great challenge to any individual to remain open in the face of so much bad news, with so much shadow and danger haunting us. We are faced with the death of the future. Matters are so complex, the scale of destruction so enormous, while the bad news seems merely to compound our sense of powerlessness, our inability to turn things around.

Faced with these enormous challenges many people lose all hope for the future. There is a feeling of having passed the point of no return, and many teenagers no longer expect to live beyond their early twenties. Many people realize how their life contributes to the destruction but feel unable to make changes, and so to protect themselves from hopelessness and fear they shut off and slip into the role of victim. They suffer the crisis as a burden, something about which they can do nothing. Overwhelmed by the responsibility, they become unable to respond.

Victim consciousness is very popular today. It is a way of opting out, but its price is a loss of vision and personal power. Having lost the capacity to deal with the crisis, we are left with the discomfort of our own fear. Our energy is then directed towards our own reaction and the crisis itself loses all meaning. We collapse into a very narrow sense of ourselves.

Crisis, however, is an integral part of life. As we have seen, in myths and legends it is the sacred wound, shattering an old condition and opening the door to a new awareness. It is a call that sets the hero on a journey of initiation. But can the old stories passed on from generation to generation provide us with a meaningful context for individual action? Can they help us to realize the inter-connectedness of our own life-journey with the story that we all share? Can they help us understand today's crisis as a challenge to mobilize our potential and rise to a new way of being? And finally, can they help us face our human shadow and re-empower ourselves to act on behalf of the larger story?

A mythic perspective can help us understand our crisis as a form of initiation. It can help to rediscover the larger story, the patterns that interconnect us with all forms of life. From a mythic perspective, our civilization has come to a threshold where the old ways of being are no longer viable. Faced with the destruction of our life-support system, we realize that our resources are finite, that we cannot go on developing and producing unlimited waste.

We have come to the end of an era where everything was centred on our human needs and wants, where we perceived ourselves as separate from nature, where we treated all other forms of life as a resource to keep the world's economies growing. Now we have reached a point where the old visions are no longer working, and we have come to realize that in order to survive we need to change our ways of being. With the power of industrialized technologies, we have set a framework for initiation. As in the old rites of initiation, we have come to a threshold where we need to leave behind an old condition, to be reborn into a new phase of our own evolution.

If we understand our current predicament as a process of initiation, a journey to a new sense of self, the images of the Grail story are very relevant. There is the land that has turned to desert, and the king who lies in agony but can neither heal nor die. Both are connected, they are a part of the same crisis. Only together can they be redeemed.

But faced with the environmental crisis we are still behaving like Parzival in the Grail Castle. We do as we have learnt, and we act in accordance with what is socially and economically acceptable. We act like perfect knights. We drive our cars and consume as we are told. Our waste is in accordance with accepted levels of toxicity, even if we know that the laws and regulations set by our governments are in no way sufficient.

And while we act in the socially accepted ways, we are failing on a deeper level. Stuck in an anthropocentric view of the world, we are out of step with the rhythms of life. As we behave in accordance with the old ways of being — while we pollute and gain control of the last resources of our planet — we are violating the realm of all future life.

Like Parzival, we are expelled into the wasteland. The Earth is turning to desert. The waters and the air are full of poisons. The forests are dying and every hour more species become extinct. In this wasteland we are called to reconnect with the flow of life. To survive we have to become agents of healing.

In the Grail Castle, Parzival was unable to reach out to the king. Confined to the narrow role of perfect knight, he was unable to ask the healing question about the nature of the king's suffering. Expelled into the wasteland he had to go through an inner process, a Rite of Passage reconnecting him with the flow of life.

When Parzival is confronted with his own shadow, his narrow identity as a knight is shattered. In the wasteland he is initiated into the realm of the heart. It is through this that he is able to heal. When he is called back to the Grail Castle he is able to reach out and ask 'What ails thee?', and thus heal the king and his land. As we awaken to the reality of the industrial wasteland we have created, we need to become ready to ask the healing questions. We, too, need to become able to reach beyond the narrow confines of our human identity to rediscover a deep sense of belonging to all of life.

Scientists are well aware of the fact that we are interdependent with all other forms of life, that we are part of the web of life of a much larger organism, planet Earth. We know that the loss of forests, the extinction of other species and the changes in the Earth's atmosphere will have an effect on us, but as yet we do not act in accordance with this knowledge. We still feel separate. Our sense of identity is still confined to a narrow human perspective.

But time is running out. As our life-support systems are turned into wasteland we are challenged to move from an old sense of who we are, to a new expanded sense of identity that includes not only all parts of ourselves, but also our fellow human beings and all other forms of life, the whole organism of which we are a part.

This shift in identity is a gigantic one. It is much more than just a change in our thinking and behaviour. It is a complete transformation in the way we experience being alive. It is moving from an understanding of ourselves as the conquerors and masters of nature (a tradition that goes back many centuries) to a sense of communion with everything that lives. To make a shift of this magnitude I believe that we need to find Rites of Passage that allow a conscious transition to a new way of being.

As I have discussed before, Rites of Passage are an important part of the cultural life of many tribal societies. They are a way of helping a person to live consciously through periods of change. This may be the transition from childhood to adult life, or the changes at the threshold to old age. As I have discussed earlier, they often involve the death of an old condition, the letting-go of an outdated vision, and a rebirth to a new expanded consciousness. But while tribal Rites of Passage are celebrated in a clear cultural context, we have no cultural context for the changes that lie ahead. We need to be creative in finding our own ways to move to a new awareness of ourselves, each other, and our relation to nature around us.

Rites of Passage can take many forms. Essentially they are experiences that evoke a deep change. They are an opportunity of bringing alive the question of 'What ails thee?', a way to live this question and to let it move us, so we can find a response deep within. As a framework for very personal experiences, such rites can transform not only our thinking but our whole way of being.

Sometimes a direct action on behalf of the natural environment can be a Rite of Passage. To stop the logging of a tropical forest by our physical presence might open our hearts to the full extent of the destruction. It might evoke grief or anger and allow us to share these feelings with others. And on a deep level it might affirm our inter-relatedness with the forests, and encourage us to shed a very narrow sense of self. It might empower us to act on behalf of other species and give us an expanded sense of identity.

Where Rites of Passage follow the patterns of initiation described earlier, they allow us to confront the threshold of death as a part of the hero's journey to a new way of being. A Rite of Passage enables us to come face to face with the threat of non-existence. It helps us to realize that our own lives and the lives of our children and future generations really are at risk. While in everyday life we are bombarded with news about the environmental crisis and the threat to our own survival, a Rite of Passage allows us to confront this threshold of death in the context of initiation. As we move beyond denial and fear, and become fully responsive to the challenges we are faced with, we can learn the lessons and realize our interrelatedness with all forms of life on our planet. To face these challenges in the framework of a Rite of Passage can prevent us from having to go through the predicted scenarios of further destruction.

In the context of a ritual, we can die to the old condition. We can become aware of the things that we have to shed. We can celebrate and honor what we have gained and learned in previous experiences, and at the same time we can recognize what is outdated and no longer current. And then, when we make changes in our lives, when we give up the luxury of driving a big car and the mindless but convenient use of resources, we are not left just with the feeling of loss. Our letting-go is then a part of the cycle of death and rebirth. Death is not the end of the future, but a necessary part of it. We are letting go of the old ways so that something newer and more vital can come to be. We are dying to the belief that we are the masters of creation and everything is at our disposal. We are letting go of the way of lonely conquerors and entering into a deep sense of inter-relatedness and belonging. We are becoming aware of the community of all species, and reconnecting with our larger story. As we open our hearts to the challenges of our times, we become able to ask the healing questions and to empower ourselves to act on behalf of all life.

The following meditation is a journey into the larger story.

Allow yourself to become relaxed — let your breath flow deeply — imagine what it would be like to open your awareness, expanding the limits of that space you call I.

Be aware of the shape of your body as it is limited by your skin. Breathe into that space, let your breath touch every part of it ... and now expand your awareness to include the space around your body, your energy field.

That, too, is you.

Let your breath expand into that space. Let this energy field around you grow. Let it expand many meters ... let it reach the size of the entire room.

Now let it expand further to reach the whole house,

town, state, country: let it include the oceans and continents until your awareness has become one with the entire planet — Gaia.

You are a wonderful green planet with water, with mountains, with rivers, trees and many thousand different forms of life — all in a delicate balance. And as you turn in space, be aware that you are a part of a much larger solar system in a galaxy in an endless, expanding universe ...

Your origins are unknown. Scientific speculation has it that you came into being as a result of a giant explosion which created the universe some 15-billion years ago. The universe may have formed from a gigantic fireball which rapidly expanded as it cooled down over many hundred-thousand years, forming countless galaxies, stars and planets. The heat of many stars remained so strong that they eventually exploded, sending interstellar dust and particles into the endless space. Over millions of years this debris formed new planets and stars, and 4.5 billion years ago out of a huge cloud of interstellar dust, our solar system may have been formed.

Time means nothing to you. It took 700,000 years for your solar system to cool down to the temperature of the sun. It was only then that the first atoms could form. And as you turned in space, you, the planet, now became an organism that was made up of many parts, of cells like stars that began to evolve ...

For a long time — for millions of years — there was silence. But within you there was the spark of creation through which you had come to be. As you turned in the endless space of the universe there was the potential to evolve ...

... After 200 million years most of your surface was covered by water. It was in the depths of the oceans that life eventually began to emerge.

As you turn in space, imagine what life would have been like for those smallest living particles which, like stars in an endless universe, began to evolve. Once life had emerged out of the smallest cells, your evolution reached a new level. It became much faster.

Within 500-million years you were to become a green planet. Plant and animal life began to spread all over you. Within a relatively short time you had become an organism, buzzing with life in thousands of different shapes and forms, each continuing to evolve and grow, each in their own way, and each as an integral part of you, Gaia, the living planet Earth.

And then, 300-million years later, something extraordinary happened: dolphins and whales who had returned to the oceans began to develop a new outer layer of the brain. This was to become the seat of higher mental functions. Together with the emergence of the first human beings 58-million years later, this may have been the dawn of consciousness. It was the beginning of a new stage in the evolution of planet Earth ...

Matter had formed out of energy, and when life emerged out of matter it had changed everything about you, the planet. And now, as life brought forth consciousness, everything was about to change again. The beginning of consciousness was an evolutionary leap which put the human species right into focus. Like no other species they began to shape life on planet Earth.

But who are we, the sons and daughters of Gaia? Within us we carry the Earth's ancient history and the seed for evolutionary leaps to come. The atoms in our bodies may have been particles in interstellar winds in the first billion years of their existence. They may have been stars in distant galaxies. Now they have come together to form you and me, our bodies, with trillions of cells all working together.

Our senses are highly specialized. We see the world, we hear it, smell it, touch it, and feel it within us. We have the ability to reflect upon ourselves and, with the capacity to anticipate the outcome of our actions, we have become a co-creator of our own destiny and the fate of planet Earth.

In the dawn of our existence the Earth seemed to provide an abundance of space. We seemed to live on a planet with endless resources, a planet that was covered with water, forests, and countless forms of plant and animal life. With the power of our minds we have created technologies, industries, cities, music, art and philosophy. We have unlocked the power of the atom, and sent satellites into space, and we have created a network of information that links the whole planet like a giant global brain. But in the course of our expansion we have altered the natural balance of life on planet Earth.

We have cleared the forests, we have polluted the air and the water. We have poisoned the Earth, and every day there are species dying — for ever. We have become ourselves an endangered species. And it is time to reflect.

As our own body is made of countless cells, like stars in a galaxy, so we are part of a much larger organism — planet Earth.

We have evolved over 15-billion years. In our genes we are still carrying that spark of creation, the ability to evolve. Now it is our consciousness that has become the stage on which evolution takes place.

The future is for us to choose ...

Bibliography

Where quoted matter within the text has no attribution, this is always taken from Wolfram von Eschenbach's *Parzival* (see below).

Beck, Peggy V. and Anna L. Walters. *The Sacred*, Navajo Community College Press, Tsaile 1977.

Boyd, Doug. *Rolling Thunder*, Random House, New York 1974.

Campbell, Joseph. *The Hero With A Thousand Faces*, Princeton University Press, Princeton 1949.

— *The Masks of God, Creative Mythology*, Penguin Books, New York 1968.

Downing, Christine. *The Goddess*, Crossroad, New York 1981.

Eliade, Mircea. *Rites and Symbols of Initiation*, Harper & Row, New York 1958.

— *The Sacred and the Profane, The Nature of Religion*, Harcourt, Brace & World Inc., New York and London 1959.

— *Myth and Reality*, Harper & Row, New York 1963.

— *Myths, Dreams and Mysteries*, Harper & Row, New York 1975.

Elkin, A.P. *Aboriginal Men of High Degree*, University of Queensland Press, St Lucia 1977.

Eschenbach, Wolfram von. *Parzival*, University of North Carolina Press, Chapel Hill 1951.

Euripides. *The Bacchae and other Plays*, Penguin Books, New York 1954.

Franz, Marie-Louise von. *Alchemy*, Inner City Books, Toronto 1980.
— *Individuation in Fairy Tales*, Spring Publications, Dallas 1980.
— *Interpretation of Fairy Tales*, Spring Publications, Dallas 1982.
— *Problems of the Feminine in Fairy Tales*, Spring Publications, Dallas 1982.
— *Shadow and Evil in Fairy Tales*, Spring Publications, Dallas 1983.
Frazer, James. *The Golden Bough*, Mentor Books, New York 1964.
Gantz, Jeffrey. *The Mabinogion*, Penguin Books, New York 1976.
Graves, Robert. *The White Goddess*, Faber & Faber, London 1948.
— *The Greek Myths*, Penguin Books, Harmondsworth 1955.
Green, Roger Lancelyn. *King Arthur*, Puffin Books, Harmondsworth 1953.
Greene, Liz. *Relating*, Samuel Weiser, New York 1977.
Grimm, Jacob and Wilhelm. *Fairy Tales*, translated by Margaret Hunt, Omega Books, Ware.
Grof, Stanislaw and Christina. *Beyond Death*, Thames & Hudson, London 1980.
Hall, Nor. *The Moon and the Virgin*, Harper & Row, New York 1980.
Harding, M. Esther. *Woman's Mysteries*, Harper & Row, New York 1971.
Harner, Michael. *The Way of the Shaman*, Harper & Row, New York 1980.
Hillman, James. *The Myth of Analysis*, Harper & Row, New York 1972.
— *Re-Visioning Psychology*, Harper & Row, New York 1975.
Houston, Jean. 'Myth and Pathos in Sacred Psychology' from *Dromenon* Vol.III, No.2, Dromenon, New York 1981.

Illich, Ivan. *Medical Nemesis*, Random House, New York 1976.

Jung, Carl Gustav. *Aion*, Bollingen Foundation, New York 1959.

Jung, Emma and Marie Louise von Franz. *The Grail Legend*, Sigo Press, Boston 1986.

Kaplan, Stuart. *Tarot Classic*, US Games Systems, New York 1972.

Kuebler-Ross, Elizabeth. *On Death and Dying*, Macmillan Publishing Co., New York 1970.

Levine, Stephen. *Who Dies?*, Anchor Books, Garden City 1982.

Malory, Thomas. *Tales of King Arthur*, Schocken Books, New York, 1982.

Matarasso, Pauline. *The Quest for the Holy Grail*, Penguin Books, Harmondsworth 1969.

Matthews, John. *The Grail, Quest for the Eternal*, Thames & Hudson, London 1981.

Meyer, Rudolf. *Zum Raum Wird Hier Die Zeit*, Urachhaus, Stuttgart 1980.

Otto, Walter F. *Dionysus, Myth and Cult*, Spring Publications, Dallas 1981.

Raffael, Burton. *Sir Gawain and the Green Knight*, Mentor Books, New York 1970.

Rebillot, Paul. *The Hero's Journey*, unpublished manuscript, Mill Valley 1981.

Samuels, Mike and Nancy. *Seeing with the Mind's Eye*, Random House/Bookworks Book, New York/Berkeley 1975.

Saxson, Linda. 'Craftsman of Chaos' from *Parabola* Vol.IV, No.1, Parabola, New York 1979.

Scholem, Gerschom G. *Major Trends in Jewish Mysticism*, Schocken Books, New York 1954.

Schult, Arthur. *Die Weltsendung des Heiligen Gral im Parzival des Wolfram von Eschenbach*, Turm, Bietigheim 1979.

Schure, Edouard. *The Great Initiates*, Rudolf Steiner Publications, New York 1961.

Singer, June. *Androgyny, Toward a New Theory of Sexuality*, Anchor Press/Doubleday, Garden City 1976.

Suzuki, Shunryu. *Zen Mind, Beginner's Mind*, John Weatherhill, New York and Tokyo 1970.

Thompson, William Irving. *The Time Falling Bodies Take to Light*, St Martin's Press, New York 1981.

Troyes, Chrestien de. *Perceval*, J.S. Brewer, Cambridge 1982.

Watts, Alan. *The Wisdom of Insecurity*, Pantheon Books, New York 1951.

— *Psychotherapy East and West*, Random House, New York 1961.

Weston, Jessie L. *From Ritual to Romance*, Cambridge University Press, Cambridge 1983.

White, T.H. *The Once and Future King*, Fontana Books, Glasgow 1962.

Whitmont, Edward C. *Return of the Goddess*, Crossroad, New York 1982.

Wosien, Maria Gabriele. *Sacred Dance*, Thames & Hudson, London 1980.

Zimmer, Heinrich. *The King and the Corpse*, Princeton University Press, Princeton 1957.

Zimmer Bradley, Marion. *The Mists of Avalon*, Alfred A. Knopf, New York 1982.

rimitive Magic

ıe Psychic Powers of
'amans and Sorcerers

nesto de Martino

HE idea of magic challenges our
basic concepts of reality and the
ural order of things. But for
ive shamans and sorcerers magic
s tangible and 'real' as science is
our modern 'civilisation'. The
tralian Aborigine, for example,
die if pierced by an arrow that
been 'sung' — no matter how
erficial the wound.

s astounding book describes
ieties where magic is a way of life,
ere sorcerers, shamans, diviners
fire walkers form powerful bonds
n the psychic realities of Nature.

MITIVE MAGIC is itself an initiation
nto the enthralling world of
ient mysteries.

ere is no such thing as unreality;
e are only various forms of
ity' — Eugene Ionesco

ERNESTO DE MARTINO lives in Rome and is Professor of the History of Religions at Cagliari University. He has a long-standing interest in the links between parapsychology and anthropology and is the author of several works in this field, including *South Italy and Magic* and *Death and Ritual in the Ancient World*.

8½ x 5½, 192 pp
Full colour cover
1 85327 021 0 Paperback

The Candle of Vision

Inner Worlds of the Imagination

A.E. (George Russell)

FOREWORD BY Nevill Drury

FIRST published in 1918, this book is one of the classics of modern western mysticism. While it may seem that such concepts as 'creative visualisation' and 'imagining our own reality' are recent innovations of the human potential movement, they are also found here — in a very lucid and eloquent form.

The author was a distinguished writer, artist and poet and believed that each of us can use the creative powers of the imagination as a pathway to other worlds. The imagination can transport us to an awesome, mystical universe and we then sense the vastness of the Infinite. This is the true nature of the visionary inspiration.

A.E. was the *nom de plume* of *GEORGE RUSSELL* (1867–1935). Russell was a major literary figure i the Irish Renaissance and a friend o W.B. Yeats. Like Yeats, Russell was strongly influenced by theosophical mysticism and by the beauty of Celtic mythology. He was the auth of several works, including *Song an its Fountains* and *The Avatars*, but CANDLE OF VISION is widely regard as his masterpiece.

8½ x 5½, 112 pp
Full colour cover
1 85327 030 X Paperback

he Celtic Twilight

·th, Fantasy and Folklore

B. Yeats

LTHOUGH renowned as one of the . most famous poets of the 20th ury, *WILLIAM BUTLER YEATS* 5–1939) was also a devoted ›nent of the western mystical and ical traditions. Yeats met with ents of the occult in Dublin in 1880s and was later introduced iis friend Charles Johnson to the osophical Society. Yeats sub-ently left the Theosophists and 890 was initiated as a ceremonial ician of the Golden Dawn — ably the most influential esoteric r in the western magical ition — and for a time became its er.

s exercised a profoundly Celtic ence on his fellow occultists and ove of Irish folklore is reflected iis book, which was first lished in 1893. THE CELTIC LIGHT brings together many of s' most enchanting and mystical tales — a dazzling array of sorcerers, faeries, ghosts and nature spirits which draw their inspiration from the visionary heart of Irish folk tradition.

This book is a special tribute to the memory of W.B. Yeats and is published fifty years after his death.

8½ x 5½, 128 pp
Full colour cover
1 85327 029 6 Paperback

Modern Ritual Magic

The Rise of Western Occultism

Francis King

THIS is the inside story of the Hermetic Order of the Golden Dawn and associated occult offshoots — told in its entirety for the first time. The author's researches into the conflict between W.B. Yeats and Aleister Crowley are described in detail, as well as the full story of Yeats' early magical training and practices. Francis King also relates the often difficult relationship between Yeats and the influential Kabbalist, Macgregor Mathers.

However, it is not only the student of the Golden Dawn who will find this book absorbing. King also describes Rudolph Steiner's attempt to take over English occultism and links Bengali Tantricism with the magic of the American Mulatto. All the major figures in modern western magic feature in this book, which since its first publication in 1970, has been rightly regarded as one of the major histories of the western esoteric tradition.

FRANCIS KING is also the author of *Magic: the Western Tradition, Sexuality, Magic and Perversion* and *The Secret Rituals of the O.T.O.* He co-authored *Techniques of High Magic* with Stephen Skinner.

8½ x 5½, 224pp
Full colour cover
1 85327 032 6

eincarnation

cient Beliefs and
odern Evidence

vid Christie-Murray

EINCARNATION is a fascinating
concept. What happens when we
Reincarnation and related
jects (such as former lives) are
easingly discussed in the media
how can the ordinary reader,
ersed in theology or psychical
arch, decide whether there is any
h in the theory?

ID CHRISTIE-MURRAY has
ered and assessed the evidence,
ries and views of reincarnation
n the religions of the East and
t, recollections of adults and
dren, mediumistic communica-
s, *déjà vu* experiences, regressive
nosis, Christos experiments, and
results of meditation techniques.

purpose is to inform, not to
ert, and after reading this book
readers should be able to reach their
own conclusions.

8½ x 5½, 288 pp
Full colour cover
1 85327 012 1 Paperback

Visionaries and Seers

They Saw Tomorrow

Charles Neilson Gattey

8½ x 5½, 288 pp
Full colour cover
1 85327 020 2 Paperback

IN this unique book, Charles Nielson Gattey recounts the stranger-than-fiction life-stories of the most astounding seers and sorcerers of all time. Such well-known characters as Nostradamus and Cheiro are here in all their brilliant and bizarre detail — including the former's visions of the Second World War and a bleak outlook for Britain towards the end of the 20th century and the latter's predictions of Edward VIII's romance and abdication — as well as such lesser-known but equally intriguing figures as Mlle Lenormande, clairvoyante and confidante of the Empress Josephine and Ernst Krafft, alleged by some to have been Hitler's personal astrologer.